Interview Yourself for Working Moms:
A Guided Journal

Interview Yourself for Working Moms:
A Guided Journal

Marci Taub

Careerstyling®, L.L.C.

Short Hills, NJ

Library of Congress Cataloging-in-Publication Data Taub, Marci, 1965–

Interview Yourself for Working Moms: A Guided Journal / Marci Taub

ISBN 0-9716785-5-3

Library of Congress Control Number: 2002090031

This book is intended as an educational and informational resource. The publisher and author expressly disclaim any responsibility or liability in connection with the use of this book.

Cover design by Cheryl Taub. Interior design by Nancy Gratton and by Publishing Professionals, New Port Richey, FL, Sylvia Hemmerly.

Cover photograph by Sardi Klein.

Careerstyling® and Interview Yourself™ are trademarks of Careerstyling®, L.L.C.

DEDICATION

This book is dedicated with unconditional love, abiding reverence, and heartfelt gratitude to my inner circle:

Adam Taub, Kyra Halle Taub, and Eli Jaron Taub, who are my beloved touchstone, my light, and my music

Arlene Karetnick, my working mom and my children's working grandmom, an extraordinary woman who makes it possible in every way for me to be a working mom

The memory of Harold Karetnick, my father, whose ethical legacy I will always cherish. He taught me the value of active listening, and inspired me with the example of his passion for both work and family

Ellyn Karetnick, my sister, who plays such a vital role in my children's lives

Cheryl and Mel Taub, my second parents, who live their lives so fully—as creative workers and as parents—that they guide and enrich everyone around them

Michelle Weichert, Michelle Tullier, Doreen DeGraaff, and Nina Greenman, working moms and enlightened souls all, who are constant sources of inspiration and support.

ACKNOWLEDGMENTS

I am grateful for the intellectual, emotional, physical, and spiritual contributions that so many people have made to this project and to my life, especially:

Nancy Gratton, my editor, for her insight, support, and creativity—all of which have made all the difference during our work together on this project.

Cheryl Taub, my cover designer, for her devoted, inspired creation; and my great production team at Publishing Professionals—especially Sylvia Hemmerly, Kathy Connor, and Leah Massie for turning my book into a reality.

Adam Taub, for his humor, friendship, patience, and loving support; Kyra and Eli, for teaching me how to be a better person—and working mom—every day; Ellyn Karetnick, for her ongoing enthusiasm about my work and for her commitment to our family; and Cheryl and Mel Taub, for their profound love and encouragement, with special thanks to Cheryl Taub for her helpful feedback at an early stage of my writing.

Steve Weichert and Philip Weiss for their professional expertise and support; Michelle Weichert, for her belief in the intrinsic value of this book, enduring friendship, optimistic outlook, and wise, loving ways; Michelle Tullier, for serving as midwife for this book, and for our long-standing professional relationship; Abbie Roth, for our magical, late-night conversations about work, family, the universe, and our spiritual journeys; Cindy Crisp, for her wise, true way of just "being"—a devoted friend and inspirational working mom; Elissa Tomasetti, for her friendship and feedback on an early table of contents; Randi Rosen, for her example as a dedicated working mom and supportive friend, and for her feedback on an early table of contents; Karen Pollack, for her gifts of thinking big, her fun-loving spirit, and her steadfast friendship; Amy McCall for her valuable input during my final stages of editing and for being a kindred writing spirit; Doreen DeGraaff, Glen Mogan, and Nancy Simpkins, who are compassionate and gifted healers; Tim Haft, whose perseverance and innovative approach to his career ventures are ongoing sources of inspiration to me; Jeanne Krier, for her public relations savvy, for teaching me many valuable lessons about her areas of expertise, and for her warm, easy-going nature that makes it a pleasure to work with her; and Phyllis Gorfain, whose many gifts—including her passion for and brilliance in her field; her leadership in interdisciplinary studies; her committed, engaging teaching; and her generous mentoring—catalyzed my interest in the power of storytelling in all of its forms and gave me the courage to challenge my assumptions; expand my intellectual boundaries; and follow my career dreams in their infancy, even when I wasn't sure how to transform my passions into concrete possibilities.

All of those people in my community, too numerous to name, whose business practices—from delivering cold medicine for my children to moving my home office furniture—make it easier for me to nurture both my family and my work.

TABLE OF CONTENTS

PREFACE

Becoming a working mom launched me on a journey of self-discovery so chaotic, so profound, that it often seems impossible to describe. I began my journey unaware of how it would challenge me again and again to create an integrated, authentic life. At each crossroads, I have engaged in a conversation with myself, reflecting on and transforming my life in ways that I hope will work for my family and me.

The Wham Factor

One of my earliest choices was to design a home-based career. In many ways, it's been my ideal scenario. No more wasted commuting time. A simplified wardrobe. And flexible work hours. But I suspect that sitcom writers are the only ones who would find my most memorable—and usually mundane—difficulties as a working mom amusing. Well, actually, as a W.A.M.U. (Worker-And-Mom-United). I'm generally not a big fan of labels. But I like this one, because it describes how I felt then—and frequently ever since—when my worker and mom roles collide: WHAM-YOU!

Distractions can appear at every turn, and at any time of the day or night. Some are welcome breaks from the ordinary. Like making up silly songs with my daughter to greet the day. Or eating breakfast under blanket tents with my son. Other distractions, though, are unwelcome. These are irritants, and they usually come in bunches. Like the time I was stuck on an endless voice-mail phone-tree while trying to fish a couple of spoons, a small red ball, and my favorite pen out of the garbage disposal with a pair of barbecue tongs, when my downstairs toilet backed up and, the baby threw up pureed pears on my shoulder. There I was, surrounded by chaos, with elevator music blaring in my ear, trying to sound professional when—at last—someone from the company I was calling finally got on the line.

Miscommunications are also inevitable. Since there's usually so much going on all at once, it's easy to make a mistake—especially when you're trying to coordinate your personal and work schedules. And some sitcom-worthy mishaps can transpire when you're trying to juggle simultaneous conversations with adults and your children—especially when you're on the phone. Children seem to know intuitively when you need to concentrate, and suddenly discover something that needs your attention right now. I remember the time I was on the phone with an office supply company representative trying to order printer paper. At a crucial point in the rep's presentation, I responded "okay, sweetie" to one of my daughter's questions, and I nearly ended up with 100 reams of paper. And I'm sure the rep was mystified by my sudden familiarity.

Identity crises—or at least identity confusions—abound as well, since working moms play so many different roles in life. Lots of times this can end up with a creative mix of the best of all your worlds. For example, I discovered that there's a kind of synergy that comes from using my working skills—like teaching and writing—when I'm involved in activities at my daughter's preschool, or from using my "mommy" skills—like mediating—to resolve work-team conflicts. Often, however, I've felt like an ambassador from another planet, trying to prove to my colleagues and clients that I'm a professional while, at times, the sounds of my children playing in the background are clearly audible over the telephone. And I repeatedly explain to family and friends how, even when I'm working at home, I'm not available for an hour-long visit.

We're All in This Together

All in all, I feel grateful for the many blessings in my life. Yet, I confess that there are moments when I obviously feel overwhelmed by my obligations as a working mom. What has really helped is to discover that I am not alone. All of the working moms I know share at least some of my challenges and pressures. We all tell trial-and-error stories about managing our work and family lives. And we all wonder—at least once a day—if there's a better way for us to design our lives. For these reasons, the story of my choices and lessons as a working mom is also the creation story of this guided journal.

A Personal Quest

Before the birth of my first child I had created a professional life that integrated career counseling, teaching, and writing. I was engaged in work that I cherished and that reflected my preference for a flexible, autonomous lifestyle. But as soon as I began to show during my first pregnancy, I started receiving lots of unsolicited questions and advice about my future life as a working mom. Most of this input consisted of variations on "You're not planning to go back to work after your baby is born, are you?" and "You'll definitely need to make special arrangements if you want to combine working and motherhood."

Outwardly, I put on a brave face. Sometimes I'd dismiss these unwelcome remarks with a laughing comment: "I suppose I'll just have to clone myself!" Other times I'd put on an optimistic front: "I'm sure I'll just know what's right when I get there." Privately, though, as my due date came nearer, I felt an increasing need to figure out just how I was going to manage the amazingly complex lifestyle that is working motherhood.

I feared that changing my work life in any way would undermine my professional credibility and limit my options for future progress. But at the same time, I truly wanted to be the best mother I could be once the baby arrived. For several weeks I allowed these fears to paralyze my decision-making process about my career direction. All I knew for sure was that I felt driven to tie up any loose ends at work prior to giving birth, so that I could start off motherhood with a clear head.

After my daughter was born, I discovered that I could feel deeply in love with her and still feel passionate about my work. But I felt overwhelmed by the challenge of how to fulfill both of these potentially all-consuming roles. I suddenly had to face many challenges related to career direction, structure, advancement, security, balance, identity, support, and energy. I especially struggled with how to direct and balance my career and life goals; get professional and personal support; and reinvent my career while maintaining my professional credibility.

At first, I searched for books about adapting your career to your lifestyle. Scanning both career and motherhood titles at my favorite bookstores, I discovered that much working mom advice was tucked into books about pregnancy or "your baby's first year." Nearly all of them seemed geared toward first-time moms, and they tended to treat working moms' lifestyle issues very superficially. Those books that did consider lifestyle issues in greater depth often focused on specialized topics, such as organizing your life or starting home-based businesses.

I finally decided to face my fears head on by asking other working moms about their own experiences in combining work and motherhood. After several conversations with others who had "been there and done that," I found out that no one had managed to come up with the perfect, one-size-fits-all solution. But there were lots of creative, piece-meal ones. And, overall, I felt relieved to discover that it would be possible to make some livable changes in my work life too, if I made those changes with care.

After dreaming and writing about some possibilities for modifying my work life, I decided to let my intuition guide me. As a first step, I prioritized time with my infant daughter in several ways: by downsizing my private practice, taking a break from teaching, and putting the finishing touches on my most recent book without making commitments to future projects. Setting attainable career and life goals, approaching my career and family lives as integrated, and adjusting my standards to reflect my priorities all helped me to achieve a sense of balance.

As a result of my decision to downsize my private practice, I needed professional support in terms of a solid referral network for current and prospective clients. I was very concerned about helping some of my current clients make smooth transitions to qualified, appropriate professionals. And it was important to forge collaborative relationships with these professionals, since I worked on a referral basis. Also, I wanted to protect my credibility by referring prospective clients to reputable colleagues. I sought advice from a mentor, and she quickly helped me to figure out the best ways for me to downsize my practice without damaging it.

On a personal level, I discovered that, in order to create time and space for my work, I needed to learn how to ask for help from family and friends. Initially, this was difficult. Like many working moms I thought that taking responsibility for my lifestyle choice meant I'd have to do it all myself. I was incredibly fortunate, however, for I discovered that there were people in my life who volunteered their help simply because it gave them pleasure. When I expressed a concern that they were doing too much, they promptly reminded me to trust them to set their own limits. From this experience I learned to seek out allies with whom I could share the challenges as well as joys of my life as a working mom.

My final set of challenges at this stage concerned reinventing my career while maintaining professional credibility. After reading about and talking with successful working moms, I realized that strengthening my connections with others would make it work. In the end, I decided to take a two-pronged approach. First, I focused on developing and maintaining key professional relationships through networking, both long-distance and in person. Second, I actively worked to maintain my visibility as a professional through my book promotion efforts, steadily giving interviews to radio shows, newspapers and magazines, and career-related web sites. All in all, this was a time of great personal growth for me and one of the most rewarding periods of my life. Little did I know that I was taking the first steps toward developing a powerful technique that I could someday share with other working moms. From these early experiences came the seeds of *Interview Yourself for Working Moms: A Guided Journal*.

The Journey Continues

These early changes made it possible for me to make the transition from career woman to working mom, but they only represented the first stage of my journey. After all, the demands of being both a professional and a mother are never static. It therefore will come as no surprise to learn that when my daughter turned one, I chose to modify my work life again—to meet both her and my changing needs.

To begin this new phase, I once again reflected on my motivations for working. I discovered that they were the same as they had been when I first started my career—I had a powerful desire both to express myself and to be of service to others. At this point in my life, though, I also needed an increasingly flexible work schedule and an escape from the high-pressure deadlines of my past.

To address these needs, I looked closely at my current situation to pinpoint just what was wrong—and what was right—about it. In addition, I realized that it was important to organize my work and home life according to my personality style. At this point in time, a writing sabbatical from my client work emerged as my most gratifying option.

This choice implied several others. For example, to truly devote myself to writing, I needed to find a way to reorganize the majority of administrative and business tasks that are related to the writing process—tasks that I once handled on my own. After researching my options, I decided that I could delegate some of these responsibilities. Likewise, I needed to develop better ways of managing the practical side of my family life. One helpful change I made in this regard was to compile a household resource directory of services and goods that I could order by phone or on-line. This allowed me to drastically reduce the amount of time I spent running errands. As a result, I was able to achieve my goals of focusing on writing and spending more time with my daughter.

Taking a writing sabbatical meant temporarily releasing the core of my pre-motherhood career. I was very apprehensive about what effect this would have on others' perceptions of my professional standing. To minimize this fear I prepared a brief explanation of my decision that I could share with whomever wanted to know what was up. During this period I also developed the habit of actively looking for spin-offs of my writing project—ways that it could tie in to my overall career goals.

Flexibility Is the Key

During my writing sabbatical I became pregnant with my second child. After my son's birth I took a brief break from my career to immerse myself in the emotional and practical transitions of my family life. During this period I greatly enjoyed helping my children bond with each other and helping my daughter adjust to her first preschool experience. I also went on a nesting craze, reorganizing my living and working spaces to best suit my new career and family needs. What once served as my home office became my daughter's new bedroom as her newborn brother took over her old room. That meant creating a new office by transforming an alcove off the family room. I devoted myself to finding creative ways to reorganize the house, adding lots of colorful bins and baskets to make it fun and easier for everyone to find and put away things.

Once I established a new routine with my family, I refocused on my writing, and found that I was ready to start phasing some client work back in, as well. In addition, I began making plans to develop and teach seminars based on my new writing projects. But throughout all this I tried to retain a clear focus, passing up some very tempting work opportunities that didn't fit well enough with my career priorities and lifestyle needs.

My toughest challenge, at this stage, was to manage my feelings. It was painful to face my fear that I wasn't giving enough—to my family or to my work. I often felt that I was trying too hard in spurts to make up for lost time and energy. I finally decided to go with the flow more, accepting that the balance between work and family would naturally shift from day to day. The key was to maintain a flexible blueprint for my work and family projects that could accommodate the constantly shifting priorities that are a part of any busy life.

Coming Full Circle

Simplifying my everyday responsibilities, setting limits, and removing guilt and overcompensation from my vocabulary helped me to navigate this third experience of adapting my career to my lifestyle. But perhaps the most important thing I did was to recognize that my needs for professional and personal support were greater and more complex than ever. My most crucial strategies were to sustain a flexible network of work and family allies, and to make time to nurture myself every day, even if just for a few minutes at a time, separate from my work and family activities.

In terms of my protecting my career credibility, I was fortunate in being able to take advantage of the dual explosion of technology and growing demand for personalized advice about issues like career and life balance, which allowed me to create a whole new approach to doing the work that I loved—an approach that was an excellent fit with my lifestyle needs.

Although it has been extremely difficult at times, both practically and emotionally, being a working mom has given me the gifts of perspective and courage to take calculated risks to balance my career and life goals; to get the professional and personal support I need; and to reinvent my career while maintaining credibility that have made both my career and life as a whole more meaningful.

Interview Yourself ™ Is Born

The story of my multiple career transformations illustrates that all of us find it challenging to be a working mom. Knowing this is what inspired me to draw on my background as both a career counselor and as a working mom to develop a special technique, the Interview Yourself™ guided-journal method for all working moms and working-moms-to-be to use.

Have you ever wished for a guidebook to help you face your overwhelming challenges as a working mom? A resource to help resolve your specific issues? An ally to help you meet your changing needs? Whether you're a working mom already or a working-mom-to-be, *Interview Yourself for Working Moms* is that dream book: an action-oriented guided journal designed just for you. It is filled with journaling tips, chapter overviews, sample entries, and 100 guided "conversations" to help you become your own career and life coach.

You may progress through the journal selectively, completing a "conversation" page, here and there, or front to back, following its thematic chapters:

- **DIRECTION:** Choose a career direction that best suits you as a working mom.
- **STRUCTURE:** Structure your career to better manage your work and family lives.
- **ADVANCEMENT:** Advance your career in ways that are compatible with your lifestyle.
- **SECURITY:** Determine how much risk is necessary for you to keep up with change.
- **BALANCE:** Achieve a sense of balance between competing demands at work and at home.
- **IDENTITY:** Integrate your worker and mom identities.
- **SUPPORT:** Develop a strong support network and become more self-reliant.
- **ENERGY:** Maximize your energy reserves while fulfilling your responsibilities.

Enhancing Working Moms' Lives

Every "conversation" is organized in the three steps of the Interview Yourself™ method—a powerful, self-directed process that will make a real difference in the quality of your life as a working mom. It guides you to: 1. *Explore* why you're stuck and what you need; 2. *Build* self-confidence about your past experience and future scenarios; and 3. *Transform* your thoughts and actions. You'll tell yourself the stories that connect your present issues, past successes, and future dreams. As you trace these connections, you'll realize scenarios for living a more balanced, authentic life. And using this method isn't intimidating. It's just like having a conversation with a wise, trusted friend who asks you relevant questions and really listens to your answers. Ultimately, you'll discover how to adapt your career to your lifestyle—at your own pace and in your own way.

Finally, your journal can help you to become aware of experiences, challenges, and ideas you can share with other working moms. In this way you, too, can contribute to alleviating some of the painful isolation that many of us feel as we get caught up in the day-to-day intensity of our busy lives. Through this process, this *Interview Yourself™* journal can become a tool for community-building among working moms and, in turn, a catalyst for social action.

Welcome to an extraordinary adventure!

Getting Started 1

A 3-Step Method
    Exploring your challenges
    Building self-confidence
    Transforming your thoughts and actions
Maximizing Your Personal Style
    Establishing your setting
    Dealing with distractions
    Making a fresh start
    Synchronizing your responses
    Maintaining your flexibility
A Guide to Help You on Your Way
A Little Philosophical Aside

L et's face it: A working mom's life is messy. There are the usual, tangible messes, like the piles of dirty laundry that threaten to climb over the edge of your hamper and stage a sit-in on your bathroom floor. And the stacks of bills peeking out of their jagged-topped envelopes, seducing you with the promise that, if you take care of them, the telephone company won't disconnect your phone and you won't max out your credit cards. And then there are the more elusive messes—the significant challenges you face whenever you find yourself at a crossroads in your life.

As much as you might dread doing your laundry or paying your bills, at least it's obvious how to clean up these messes. It's the other kind of messes that can really keep you up at night, pacing the bedroom floor. Messes like: **How can I design a more integrated, meaningful, authentic life as a working mom?**

The growing volume and conflicting nature of advice about how to deal with such lifestyle issues can cause even the most ambitious multi-tasker to feel overloaded and confused. Sure, there are handbooks that cover some of these issues. But many of these books are only for certain kinds of working moms and only provide generic solutions that don't necessarily apply to your situation.

Interview Yourself for Working Moms takes an entirely different approach. This book is for all kinds of working moms and working moms-to-be. "Working moms," include: part-timers (traditional and job-sharers); full-timers (traditional and flex-timers); home-based workers (telecommuters, entrepreneurs, and free agents); organization-based workers (in all sectors and career fields); and field-based workers (rovers who move from one temporary office or location to another). "Working moms-to-be," include: expecting-mom workers (first-time moms-to-be); re-enterers (moms who are planning to go back to work after focusing exclusively on being moms for any period of time); newly-minted workers (moms who are planning to go to work for the first time); and fence-sitters (moms who are considering going back to work or to work for the first time).

This book is a guided journal that shows you how to talk to yourself about your particular needs and obstacles. And it's based on the premise that if you talk to yourself constructively, you can enhance your life. Through the process of writing down relevant, specific stories about yourself, you can discover what means most to you, what's standing between you and your goals, and how to overcome these obstacles to achieve the lifestyle best suited to your needs. And, because the Interview Yourself™ method is a self-paced, personal journey of discovery, it isn't intimidating. Instead, it's just like having a conversation with a wise, trusted friend—a friend who asks you relevant questions and really listens to your answers, guiding you to enhance your life.

The Interview Yourself™ method is more than a story-telling venture. To get the most out of this technique there are some important guidelines to learn and put into practice. So before we move on to the guided conversations, let's take a moment to delve into the process.

A 3-Step Method

The majority of this book is made up of a series of guided conversations, grouped together in eight thematic chapters: Direction, Structure, Advancement, Security, Balance, Identity, Support, and Energy. When you're struggling with how to realign your work and personal lives, you can choose a relevant chapter and work through its series of conversations.

And, while the guided conversations are thematically organized, they can also stand alone. If you just want to work on a particular issue, you can turn to a related conversation. Whether you progress from "Conversation #1" straight through to "Conversation #100" or travel a more eclectic path, sampling a few conversations from chapter 4, a few from chapter 8, and then a few from chapter 2, it's important to remember that there are three basic steps that underlay the Interview Yourself™ method.

Exploring your challenges

Step One involves introspection. In the guided conversations, this step is initiated through the **Explorers** questions. These questions are probing, and they're designed to help you discover why you may be stuck on a particular issue or concept. Within the **Explorers** sections there are two subsets of questions that are tailored to the specific needs of the conversation you're working on.

Building self-confidence

Step Two involves building self-confidence. This is accomplished through the **Confidence-Builders** questions. Here you'll find a couple of question subsets, entitled **Life Lessons** and **Potential Outcomes**, respectively. Each of these question sets is designed to address your possible fears and confusion by assessing your resources and putting your risk of change into perspective.

Transforming your thoughts and actions

Step Three involves considering a new approach to your situation. You do this through the **Transformers** questions in each conversation. Here you'll find two **Talk-Over** opportunities. These are invitations to examine your current beliefs and behaviors in light of their influence on your ability to achieve your desired goals. Through your responses to these **Talk-Over** questions, you'll replace negative, self-inhibiting attitudes and actions with positive, self-actualizing ones.

Maximizing Your Personal Style

By conscientiously working through these three steps, you can make your journaling experience a powerful tool for self-development. As you evolve through the many different stages of your life, the Interview Yourself ™ method can help you to maintain the creativity, flexibility, and adaptability that will enrich your every day.

It's important to remember that there's no one right way to go about using this method. What matters is that you respect your personal journaling style. The following sections will show you just a few of the ways that you can tailor this process to your personal style.

Establishing your setting

When and where you use your journal can make a big difference in the quality of your experience. Some people need a regular routine—a particular time and place that's dedicated specifically to journaling. Others require more variety.

To find out what's right for you, imagine yourself in an ideal setting for the journaling process. Do you see yourself contentedly curled up in bed late at night, or sitting beneath a big old tree in the local park in the late afternoon? Does it feel more comfortable to envision yourself at your desk during your lunch hour, or at the kitchen table in the cool quiet of early morning?

Now, take these questions deeper. As a working mom you're likely to find it difficult to keep any particular time and place free from interruption all the time. So, once you've identified your ideal journaling conditions, select those elements that seem most appealing to you. For example, is the place more important than the time? Do you feel that silence is an absolute must, or does gentle music or the sounds of nature seem to be necessary before you can truly get into the self-interviewing process? Even seemingly minor considerations of temperature and lighting can make a difference to your journaling experience.

Dealing with distractions

No matter where and when you choose to conduct your self-interviews, there's always going to be something that catches your attention, beckons to be addressed, or pulls you in, whether you want it to or not. And even when external distractions are absent, there are some issues that will arise during the Interview Yourself ™ process that will present you with challenges that, themselves, can threaten to distract you from your ultimate goal.

Remember that keeping this journal is not intended to become a chore. Rather, it should be a gift you give to yourself—a joyous experience of self-discovery and problem-solving. One way to make this an uplifting experience is to alternate long stretches—if time permits—with short sessions. Long stretches afford you the luxury of really thinking through your ideas and feelings in greater depth. Short sessions, on the other hand, can take the pressure off, allowing you to jump in and get a few quick thoughts down on paper (or tape).

And when you're especially busy, here's a useful trick. Pick a relevant conversation question and keep it in the back of your mind for a few days. Just let your subconscious work on it for awhile. You may be surprised to discover that while you're preoccupied with your daily activities, you're also generating creative responses to the question—seemingly without even trying.

Making a fresh start

If you're like most of us, you've probably have had at least one negative experience with writing or journaling. Perhaps you've felt that you didn't have good-enough writing skills. Or you were daunted by the idea of having to make a regular commitment to writing. Or you felt that you had nothing worthwhile to say. And, for many of you, the prospect of actually facing your problems may, itself, be intimidating.

The Interview Yourself ™ method is designed to help you avoid such problems. You aren't expected to confront a blank page and spontaneously fill it with confessions from the depths of your soul. Instead, each conversation provides guidance through questions and examples. It's an action-oriented approach, intended to focus your thoughts on particular issues and goals.

To get the most out of the process, you need to give yourself permission to speak freely to yourself. This means learning to explore your innermost feelings—even the messy, conflicted ones—without judging or censoring any of them before, during, or after you record them. If you find it difficult to get this free flow of self-knowledge started, here are a few preliminary exercises you can try:

1. *Take an Inner Sight-Seeing Tour*: Focus on your visions by drawing pictures, day-dreaming, or meditating. Once you've selected a conversation question to work on, jot down your initial impressions. Use word associations or poetry if they seem to help. If you're having trouble organizing your thoughts, try writing out your ideas on individual pieces of paper and rearranging them in groups until you find a combination that reflects your sense of priorities.

2. *Tune Into Your Inner Radio*: Listen to your answers by discussing them with yourself quietly or out loud, tape recording your discussions with yourself to play back at a later time, or singing a song.

3. *Join Your Inner Circus*: Stir up your reactions by clowning or playing around. Dance to your favorite music, drum your fingers, tap your feet, go for a quick jog or bike ride. Or try play-acting the different options suggested by a particular conversation question.

Synthesizing Your Responses

Use both your intellect and your intuition to work through your ideas and your feelings. Listen attentively to yourself, then try to summarize what you've discovered as concisely as possible. This will help you to expose areas where your thoughts and feelings are conflicted. But don't pressure yourself to immediately resolve such conflicts. Instead, explore them thoroughly. Try posing your options to yourself like this: "One way to look at my situation is . . . , but another way to see it would be. . . ." Or "It sounds like what I want is . . . , and at the same time I hear myself saying. . . ." Or "A part of me believes that I'm stuck because. . . . , and a different part of me feels that the real reason is. . . ."

At all times, let your intuition guide you. Find significant patterns in your responses by reading between the lines, listening for what resonates as most true for you, or connecting with what options feel in synch with where you're at in your life. Trust what you learn about yourself intuitively, and avoid the temptation to dismiss your discoveries as silly or off-base just because they may differ from what you expect yourself to think or feel.

Maintaining Your Flexibility

Life is a process of constant change. That's why your ideal career and life balance, as well as the things you need to do to achieve your goals, will change many times over the course of your life as a working mom. Sometimes this inevitability of change—and the pace at which change occurs—can feel overwhelming. At such times it's understandable for you to want to just stop working on your journal.

If you find yourself tempted to pull back from journaling through your issues, recognize that your goal is to stay grounded in the present—to deal with the issues facing you today. As you accumulate positive experiences through self-interviewing you'll develop greater confidence to explore and transform future challenges, enriching both your career and your overall lifestyle.

A Guide to Help You on Your Way

As those of you who've kept either a conventional or guided journal know, we all feel stuck sometimes. To make it easier for you to get and keep going, I've included "shadow journaler" entries on the left hand pages of each conversation. These responses are based on my own experiences from when, like you, I stood at a crossroads, facing tough issues as a working mom.

My entries are meant only as a source of companionship and inspiration for you. Please know that your answers can—and no doubt will—be very different from mine. Consider my comments, in addition to the guidelines I've offered in this chapter, as jump-starters for whenever you find yourself stuck on a particular conversation question.

A Little Philosophical Aside

Before you begin your journaling experience, I'd like to share with you ten philosophical principles that have guided my client work and my development of the Interview Yourself ™ method:

1. *Know your "career"*: "Career" now includes every role that you play in all aspects of your life, making all of them—big and small; short-term and long-term; in paid work, hobbies, and personal relationships—real and connected in your lifelong process of self-development;

2. *Discover fulfillment*: Meaningful work that reflects your passions, talents, values, personality, and lifestyle is vital to living an authentic, rewarding life;

3. *Create chances*: Opportunities for meaningful work arise when you use specific strategies like keeping an open mind and networking;

4. *Make choices*: Choices among meaningful roles, jobs, and career fields are abundant, and the real challenge is deciding what to do when;

5. *Design your path*: Pathways leading in many different directions will help you to make your choices into realities and to adapt them to your lifestyle, and sometimes the best paths are the offbeat, spontaneous ones;

6. *Take risks*: Risks are a necessary part of change and growth, and, when you're at a crossroads, it's important to assess how much risk you need and feel comfortable taking financially, intellectually, emotionally, physically, and spiritually;

7. *Remain flexible*: Plans that integrate your career and life goals flexibly will reduce your stress and increase your ability to balance the many demands on your time and energy;

8. *Nurture yourself*: Approaches that are holistic—nurturing your mind, body, and spirit—are essential for successfully adapting your career to your lifestyle;

9. *Embrace your lifecycles*: Cycles of loss and renewal are inevitable as you grow, change, and reinvent yourself, and you need both to grieve the losses and to celebrate the renewals to evolve spiritually; and

10. *Become a storyteller*: Life stories—both those you tell yourself and those you share with others—are powerful ways to learn fundamental truths about yourself, connect with and build communities with others, and pass on legacies of values to future generations.

So, with these principles in mind, let's begin the conversation. . . .

DIRECTION: Going From Here

2

The Conversations
- Getting the inside story
- Doing it your way
- Prioritizing why you work
- Seeing if the shoe still fits
- Exploring the right stuff
- Asking the board
- Targeting the final three
- Looking under the bed and in the closets
- Getting to heaven by looking down
- Going with the flow
- Believing that size doesn't matter
- Counting three, two, one, lift-off

M ost of us were brought up to think of "real" work in traditional ways: as paid employment outside the home, as demanding a full-time commitment, as somehow different—and maybe even more important—than our other regular, vital, yet unpaid activities. But these traditional ideas of work are often inappropriate for working moms.

Changing Assumptions about Work

The problem is that we tend to judge ourselves and our successes by the standards we've learned while we were growing up. So we often neglect to give ourselves credit for our career accomplishments if we achieve them outside of a conventional context, like an office. And we frequently fail to recognize that there are unconventional ways to accomplish many of the same goals that we have, up to now, worked toward in more traditional ways.

For example, traditional jobs generally assume a fixed time commitment: 9-to-5, five days a week is the most common, but there are lots of variations on this theme. And traditional jobs commonly require that you spend that time in an environment over which the employer, not the employee, has the greatest amount of control. But as a working mom, you'll probably discover that you have a greater need for autonomy and flexibility than traditional jobs allow. To gain that autonomy and flexibility, you may have to seek creative new ways to accomplish your tasks both at work and at home. You may discover that it's more convenient to reorganize the way you schedule your work. You may even find it worthwhile to redefine your work. Your challenge, then, is to re-evaluate your assumptions about what constitutes "real" work, as a first step toward adapting your career to your lifestyle.

Awakening Your Creativity

In the twelve conversations that follow, you'll open yourself to a more creative definition of who you are at work and at home. Each conversation moves you toward discovering a more satisfying approach to your career, and by the end of this chapter, you'll have made real progress toward surpassing the limitations imposed by traditional ideas of work.

Your goal during these twelve journal entries is to view all of your skills and attributes as potential assets. As you re-evaluate your talents, needs, and preferences, you'll learn that there are many different ways to employ them.

Dig deep into your experiences and feelings as you engage in these conversations about choosing a career direction that best suits you as a working mom. Turn your imagination loose and dare to envision your ideal life. And if you're baffled by any of the questions, you can always look at how I approached them, because my journal entries are right beside yours.

Conversation #1: Getting The Inside Story

Explorers

Real Work: What counts as "real work" to you?

> My parents taught me that "real work" includes everything that you do to contribute to your family and community—both financially and emotionally. But sometimes I find myself undervaluing the work I do outside of my paid work.

Career Changes: Under what conditions can you imagine yourself making career changes?

> I would make a change if my work and home life came into conflict with each other. Being the mother of two young children has motivated me to find more flexible ways of pursuing my writing, counseling, and teaching passions.

Confidence-Builders

Life Lessons: What 3 times have you felt good about yourself as a result of doing what you considered to be "real work" or making some kind of career change?

> Getting published the first time gave me a creative thrill and let me help many other people. Becoming a parent let me share myself fully and taught me to approach life with joy and gratitude. And pursuing an independent combination of counseling, writing and teaching let me integrate all three passions into one balanced life.

Potential Outcomes: What's the worst thing that could happen if you made a career change now? What's the best thing that could happen?

> The worst things would be that my income would become less predictable and that there could be new demands on my time and energy that I couldn't handle. The best thing would be that my decision launches a highly gratifying new phase of my career.

Transformers

Talk-Over #1: How can you talk to yourself in a new way about "real work" that gives you a more flexible approach to directing your career?

> I can say: "Different aspects of my real work can be more important to me than others at certain points in my life. And it's okay if my feelings change about what means most to me and about how many—or how few—roles I can handle at once."

Talk-Over #2: How can you talk to yourself in a new way about making career changes that gives you a more flexible approach to directing your career?

> I can say: "I'm not alone—there are others who have faced similar choices and I can turn to them for advice and support."

Conversation #1: Getting The Inside Story

Explorers

Real Work:

Career Changes:

Confidence-Builders

Life Lessons:

Potential Outcomes:

Transformers

Talk-Over #1:

Talk-Over #2:

Conversation #2: Doing It Your Way

Explorers

Typical Lifestyle: What are the pros and cons of the typical lifestyle in your chosen work?

> I enjoy the flexibility that comes with working from my home office, from scheduling to dress code. On the other hand, I now have a longer commute to my teaching job, and it can be hard to make myself focus on work at home when I can hear the rest of the family having fun.

Alternative Ways to Work: What alternative ways to work do you favor?

> I prefer flexible work hours so that I can make last minute schedule adjustments whenever my family's needs demand it. I'd like to work out of my home as much as possible during the weekdays so that I can weave my work and personal schedules together with as little hassle as possible.

Confidence-Builders

Life Lessons: What 3 times have you felt good about yourself as a result of shaping your work life to fit your lifestyle?

> The changes that have allowed me more time to pursue family and educational interests have given me the most satisfaction. Taking flexible interim jobs let me enroll in a certificate program, transferring my practice to my home office gave me time for my family, and taking a sabbatical to write let me cut down on personal and professional stress when my family needed me the most.

Potential Outcomes: What's the worst thing that could happen if you adapted your career to your lifestyle now? What's the best thing that could happen?

> The worst thing would be that, by relying heavily on e-mail and faxes, I'd lose too much face-to-face contact with colleagues and clients. On the other hand, the best would be that I can more completely integrate my work life with my personal life.

Transformers

Talk-Over #1: How can you talk to yourself in a new way about your work's typical lifestyle that gives you a more flexible approach to directing your career?

> I can say: "I have a freedom in my work lifestyle that gives me time to take care of myself and my family."

Talk-Over #2: How can you talk to yourself in a new way about alternative ways to work that gives you a more flexible approach to directing your career?

> I can say: "I have complete control to better my work situation, as long as I remember to do a few key things—like making realistic writing deadlines—so that I can enjoy both my work and my family."

Conversation #2: Doing It Your Way

Explorers

Typical Lifestyle:

Alternative Ways to Work:

Confidence-Builders

Life Lessons:

Potential Outcomes:

Transformers

Talk-Over #1:

Talk-Over #2:

Conversation #3: Prioritizing Why You Work

Explorers

Reasons to Work: What are the top three reasons for why you work?

> My three main reasons for working are: I need a way to express myself creatively, I want to help people improve the quality of their lives, and I need to contribute to my family's income.

The Big Payoff: Does what you get out of your work justify doing it? Why or why not?

> To some extent, my work meets my top three needs. But I believe that it could be more satisfying if I allow myself to change focus when it's necessary. I'm not 100 percent sure, but right now it may be better for me to spend more time writing and teaching, and less time on client work.

Confidence-Builders

Life Lessons: What 3 times have you felt good about yourself as a result of making career choices driven by your most important reasons to work?

> Earning my master's degree in counseling, creating and teaching career development courses, and getting my third book published all allowed me to build on the foundations I had in my three career passions while letting me continue to work in all of my chosen fields.

Potential Outcomes: What's the worst thing that could happen if you matched your career choices with your career values now? What's the best thing that could happen?

> I'm afraid that spending more time teaching than working with clients will lead to others seeing me as more of a teacher and writer than as a counselor, but if I can integrate the three parts of my work well, I could make an even greater contribution to the community while still meeting my obligations to my family.

Transformers

Talk-Over #1: How can you talk to yourself in a new way about your reasons to work that gives you a more flexible approach to directing your career?

> I can say: "To satisfy myself I need to start a new creative project at least once a year, while still writing, teaching, and counseling about issues that are related to making people's lives better."

Talk-Over #2: How can you talk to yourself in a new way about the big payoff that gives you a more flexible approach to directing your career?

> I can say: "It is most important to listen to my own instincts about what I need from my work rather than listening to what other people might think is important."

Conversation #3: Prioritizing Why You Work

Explorers

Reasons to Work:

The Big Payoff:

Confidence-Builders

Life Lessons:

Potential Outcomes:

Transformers

Talk-Over #1:

Talk-Over #2:

Conversation #4: Seeing If The Shoe Still Fits

Explorers

Work Interests and Skills: What about your work makes you look forward to doing it on a regular basis?

> I look forward to working every day because I enjoy facilitating self-exploration, brainstorming possibilities, synthesizing vast quantities of information, motivating others, and collaborating with others while exploring my strongest interests, which all relate to self-development.

Personality Attributes: Which of your favorite attributes help you to succeed in your work? Which of your favorite attributes are somewhat or totally irrelevant to your work?

> My favorite attributes that help me to succeed in my work are intuition, optimism, adaptability, tenacity, empathy, and charisma. At this point, all of these things have helped me in my work.

Confidence-Builders

Life Lessons: What 3 times have you felt good about yourself as a result of doing work that maximized what you like and who you are?

> When I've successfully used my favorite skills as a career counselor I've felt good about being able to assist my clients. Teaching a course for prospective mental health professionals was another instance when I got to fully indulge in what I enjoy, using my personal style. And I felt really good about myself while I was writing my third book, because it called upon many of my talents, interests, and attributes.

Potential Outcomes: What's the worst thing that could happen if you focused on your favorite work interests, skills, and personality attributes now? What's the best thing that could happen?

> The worst thing that could happen would be that I neglect other, necessary tasks while indulging only those things that I find more satisfying. The best thing is that I could find myself more fulfilled in my career, and that this would spill over into the rest of my life.

Transformers

Talk-Over #1: How can you talk to yourself in a new way about your favorite work interests and skills that moves you toward a more flexible approach to directing your career?

> I can say: "Truly enjoying my work means that I need to spend my time doing what I love to do in a way that works with my personality so that it is a fully involved experience for me."

Talk-Over #2: How can you talk to yourself in a new way about your favorite personality features that moves you toward a more flexible approach to directing your career?

> I can say: "I'm most likely to succeed at work when I play to my strengths as much as possible and find new ways to apply them to my work."

Conversation #4: Seeing If The Shoe Still Fits

Explorers

Work Interests:

Personality Attributes:

Confidence-Builders

Life Lessons:

Potential Outcomes:

Transformers

Talk-Over #1:

Talk-Over #2:

Conversation #5: Exploring The Right Stuff

Explorers

Generating Possibilities: What other professions have you considered or fantasized about? Why haven't you actively pursued them?

> I've considered being an educational software developer, a curriculum and instructional design specialist, the author of a series of guided journals about self-development and lifestyle issues and the developer of a related seminar series. I haven't actively pursued these professions partly because I haven't yet figured out which attracts me most or how to make them happen.

Fact-Finding Missions: How did you discover these other professions? What steps, if any, have you taken to find out more about them?

> I read about educational software development in magazine articles. I explored it by talking with people in related fields. I got interested in curriculum and instructional design while teaching. I happened upon the profession of guided-journal author when I was trying to pull all my interests into one career and have been exploring what this fantasy career might actually be like in reality.

Confidence-Builders

Life Lessons: What 3 times have you felt good about yourself as a result of exploring other careers?

> I felt good about myself when I checked out placement counseling as a possible career development profession. It was not an ideal fit for me, I was able to get a better idea of the kind of approach that I wanted to aim for. When I interviewed for a full-time training position, I learned that my interviewers recognized me as a professional colleague with a lot to offer. Finally, my job as an executive education consultant let me collaborate with many gifted people who shared work styles and goals with me.

Potential Outcomes: What's the worst thing that could happen if you explored a range of possible careers now? What's the best thing that could happen?

> The worst thing would be that I'd spread myself too thin—I tend to do that a lot. The best thing would be to clarify my best next move and feel comfortable that I'd made an informed decision.

Transformers

Talk-Over #1: How can you talk to yourself in a new way about your work possibilities that gives you a more flexible approach to directing your career?

> I can say: "The types of work that I might enjoy at different stages in my career will change."

Talk-Over #2: How can you talk to yourself in a new way about your fact-finding missions that gives you a more flexible approach to directing your career?

> I can say: "I give myself permission to find out more about professions that interest me, because exploring my options doesn't commit me to anything until I'm truly ready to make a change."

Conversation #5: Exploring The Right Stuff

Explorers

Generating Possibilities:

Fact-Finding Missions:

Confidence-Builders

Life Lessons:

Potential Outcomes:

Transformers

Talk-Over #1:

Talk-Over #2:

Conversation #6: Asking The Board

Explorers

Your Career Advisory Board: Whom specifically do you usually turn to for advice about your career direction? Do you usually consult with too few, too many, or just the right number of people?

> When I'm at a career crossroads, I usually ask my husband, my mentor, and my best friend for advice. I usually ask for just the right amount of advice. But sometimes I try to figure things out too much on my own.

The Agenda: What kind of advice about your career direction have you found to be helpful? What kind of advice has been counterproductive?

> The most helpful advice is usually specific and related to how to accomplish my goals—how to make a career change, how to maintain my professional credibility, or how to navigate around the emotional pitfalls that I may encounter. Advice that is less helpful tends to be very general: "There's really only one right way to do something," for example.

Confidence-Builders

Life Lessons: What 3 times have you felt good about yourself as a result of taking career advice from others?

> When I decided to modify my career after my first child was born, I discussed my options with my husband and he helped me figure out how to break the problem down and then focus on solving it piece by piece. That helped me clarify my priorities and find specific ways to make them happen. When I turned to my mentor for practical advice on how to downsize my private practice, she taught me how to handle client referrals, so that I could make my transition without damaging my credibility. I've also turned to my best friend for advice on how to deal with feeling torn between work and family obligations. After all, she'd been through something like this herself.

Potential Outcomes: What's the worst thing that could happen if you solicited constructive input from others about your career whenever you're at a crossroads? What's the best thing that could happen?

> The worst would be that I might get more confused about what to do—from hearing conflicting opinions, or feeling unduly influenced by someone else. The best thing that could happen is that my advisory board could help me explore my options and figure out what is best for me.

Transformers

Talk-Over #1: How can you talk to yourself in a new way about your career advisory board that gives you a more flexible approach to directing your career?

> I can say: "My advisors are an important resource for me as I develop my career choices that gives me strength by using it, rather than showing weakness."

Talk-Over #2: How can you talk to yourself in a new way about your agenda that gives you a more flexible approach to directing your career?

> I can say: "People who give me specific and relevant advice are the most helpful. I will seek them out whenever I need help in focusing and directing my life."

Conversation #6: Asking The Board

Explorers

Your Career Advisory Board:

The Agenda:

Confidence-Builders

Life Lessons:

Potential Outcomes:

Transformers

Talk-Over #1:

Talk-Over #2:

Conversation #7: Targeting The Final Three

Explorers

The Usual Suspects and Newcomers: What three professions have emerged as your top choices? What makes these choices seem best for your current needs?

> Writing, teaching, and counseling have emerged as my top three choices—especially if I can combine them creatively. All three are long-term interests of mine, and by integrating them into a single career, I can pursue them all simultaneously.

Realistic vs. Settling: Are each of these three choices primarily appealing only because you believe that you can handle them, or because they truly challenge you?

> All of my choices appeal to me because they challenge me to use my gifts to the fullest. I'm confident that I can achieve my goals.

Confidence-Builders

Life Lessons: What 3 times have you felt good about yourself as a result of making or fantasizing about career choices that were both exciting and attainable?

> When I was younger, I often fantasized about becoming a world-class skater. I learned to believe that it's always possible to find—and do—work that I feel passionate about. Choosing to become a career counselor was another confidence-building experience—I woke up every morning eager to go to work. My lifelong fantasy about becoming a writer drove me to find a way to make it happen. When I finally published my first book, it felt great to realize that I had made my dream come true.

Potential Outcomes: What's the worst thing that could happen if you pursued your top long-term or newly-discovered career choice now? What's the best thing that could happen?

> The worst thing would be to find out that my "dream" career turns out to be less fulfilling than I had expected. The best thing would be to discover that I've come up with a really rewarding new career that I can continue to evolve with so that it remains gratifying over the long term.

Transformers

Talk-Over #1: How can you talk to yourself in a new way about your career choices that gives you a more flexible approach to directing your career?

> I can say: "Career choices that reflect who I really am today inevitably will change as I grow. But the seeds of my interests most likely will reappear in my new choices."

Talk-Over #2: How can you talk to yourself in a new way about what's realistic vs. settling that gives you a more flexible approach to directing your career?

> I can say: "Finding a truly satisfying career sometimes involves the courage to step away from the tried-and-true and explore new directions. There's real excitement and satisfaction in using my gifts in a new, creative way."

Conversation #7: Targeting The Final Three

Explorers

The Usual Suspects and Newcomers:

Realistic vs. Settling:

Confidence-Builders

Life Lessons:

Potential Outcomes:

Transformers

Talk-Over #1:

Talk-Over #2:

Conversation #8: Looking Under The Bed And In The Closets

Explorers

Decision-Making Fears: What are your main career decision-making fears?

> I'm afraid of not making the best decision possible—of being too short-sighted to see opportunities or of settling for less than I could really achieve. I'm also aware that I've got a kind of fear of success: whenever I accomplish something, I'm worried that I won't be able to top it next time.

Fear Triggers: What usually triggers your fears?

> When I find myself approaching a career decision too intensely, I notice that my fear of not making the best decision possible kicks in. I also notice that it's usually just before I have to commit myself to making a change that I start showing signs that my fear of success is acting up.

Confidence-Builders

Life Lessons: What 3 times have you felt good about yourself as a result of facing your career decision-making fears?

> When I made the transition into private practice I took several interim positions that offered me some flexibility. This enabled me to deal with my fear of not making the right decision by letting me work up the courage to take the final plunge. Whenever I take on a new book project I'm always worried that I won't be able to match the success of my last effort. By taking a deep breath, and focusing on the task at hand, I can banish my fears long enough to get the writing done. During my sabbatical, I was afraid that such a break focused soley on writing would jeopardize my career status. But I could always remind myself that it was just a short-term change, and that I could go back to the other aspects of my career any time I chose.

Potential Outcomes: What's the worst thing that could happen if you faced your fears and made a career decision now? What's the best thing that could happen?

> The worst thing that could happen is that I feel pressured—by both myself and others—to succeed immediately and on a grand scale. The best thing would be to find that I can overcome my fears and commit to a career change that ultimately will be hugely satisfying.

Transformers

Talk-Over #1: How can you talk to yourself in a new way about your decision-making fears that gives you a more flexible approach to directing your career?

> I can say: "Admitting to my fears lets me put them in perspective, and that lets me keep them from taking over my life."

Talk-Over #2: How can you talk to yourself in a new way about your fear triggers that gives you a more flexible approach to directing your career?

> I can say: "Looking at my fears honestly will teach me valuable lessons about how I work, which will let me become more efficient and capable as I work."

Conversation #8: Looking Under The Bed And In The Closets

Explorers

Decision-Making Fears:

Fear Triggers:

Confidence-Builders

Life Lessons:

Potential Outcomes:

Transformers

Talk-Over #1:

Talk-Over #2:

Conversation #9: Getting To Heaven By Looking Down

Explorers

Going to Extremes: Concerning your career goals, how do you define "short-term" and "long-term"?

> My short-term goals are those that I hope to accomplish within a year, while my long-term career goals are those that I hope to accomplish within three years.

Sacrificial Offerings: How much time, energy, and money are you willing and able to invest now toward achieving your short- and long-term career goals?

> I'm willing to cut back on "extras"—take shorter or less elaborate vacations, for example, if that's what it takes to reach my goals. I am not willing, however, to compromise the time I give to my family, and I'm not willing to force them to skimp on their needs to support my career.

Confidence-Builders

Life Lessons: What 3 times have you felt good about yourself as a result of making progress toward achieving your career goals?

> I celebrated passing the one-year mark in my private practice, because it meant that I'd come far in establishing myself in that new phase of my career. Achieving my short-term goal of setting up new computer systems to manage every aspect of my private practice, made me proud of the new level of professional efficiency I had achieved. Mid-way through my writing sabbatical, I felt that I'd made a breakthrough in both the content and style of my writing—this felt good because I'd succeeded in using a short-term choice to powerfully boost my longer-term career plans.

Potential Outcomes: What's the worst thing that could happen if you took steps to make your career goals and strategies to achieve them attainable now? What's the best thing that could happen?

> The worst thing that could happen is that I could learn that my judgment was way off about what is realistic to achieve and how to do it. The best thing is that I could find myself taking comfortable steps toward my career goals and feeling good about my progress along the way.

Transformers

Talk-Over #1: How can you talk to yourself in a new way about going to extremes that gives you a more flexible approach to directing your career?

> I can say: "There are always options. There is no situation that I need to feel trapped in, as long as I give myself the personal power to take changes in stride."

Talk-Over #2: How can you talk to yourself in a new way about sacrificial offerings that gives you toward a more flexible approach to directing your career?

> I can say: "Making a short term sacrifice to achieve my goals can only result in long-term satisfaction when the job is done."

Conversation #9: Getting To Heaven By Looking Down

Explorers

Going to Extremes:

Sacrificial Offerings:

Confidence-Builders

Life Lessons:

Potential Outcomes:

Transformers

Talk-Over #1:

Talk-Over #2:

Conversation #10: Going With The Flow

Explorers

Connecting with Intuition: How do you usually tune in to your intuition's guidance?

> My intuition makes itself known physically. Sometimes I'll feel a sudden little chill, or a hot flash, a headache, or feel sick to my stomach—that's my inner wisdom alerting me that something's not quite right. By contrast, I know I'm intuitively on the right track when I feel a deep sense of inner peace and very grounded—as if I'm in synch with myself and with all that's around me.

Second Guessing Yourself: Do you usually make important decisions in your life primarily by thinking them through or by trusting your instincts? Once you've made these decisions, are you usually comfortable with them, or do you second-guess yourself?

> I usually make important decisions in my life primarily by trusting my instincts. Once I've made them, I'm often okay to move on with them, but sometimes I second-guess myself and retreat into my intellectual mode to overanalyze my decisions.

Confidence-Builders

Life Lessons: What 3 times have you felt good about yourself as a result of trusting your intuition about career decisions?

> When I began my certificate program in adult career development and planning, I felt certain that this was the right career move. On another occasion my intuition warned me to turn down some potentially lucrative opportunities during my writing sabbatical. Finally, collaborating on a book with a close colleague was an intuitive decision that worked out in both of our best interests.

Potential Outcomes: What's the worst thing that could happen if you trusted your intuition about your career needs now? What's the best thing that could happen?

> The worst thing that could happen is that I let my fears block my intuitive navigator and I get a little lost in finding my career direction. The best thing that could happen is that I follow my intuition and it clearly steers me in the right direction.

Transformers

Talk-Over #1: How can you talk to yourself in a new way about connecting with intuition that gives you a more flexible approach to directing your career?

> I can say: "My intuition is a valuable tool for directing my career that I should use for every decision I make, big or small."

Talk-Over #2: How can you talk to yourself in a new way about second-guessing yourself that gives you a more flexible approach to directing your career?

> I can say: "Thinking through my decisions by truly listening to myself—and therefore my intuition—will minimize my self-doubt and increase my confidence in making a decision."

Conversation #10: Going With The Flow

Explorers

Connecting with Intuition:

Second Guessing Yourself:

Confidence-Builders

Life Lessons:

Potential Outcomes:

Transformers

Talk-Over #1:

Talk-Over #2:

Conversation #11: Believing That Size Doesn't Matter

Explorers

Leftover Needs: Which of your needs can't be met or met fully by your career choice?

> My main unmet need would be daily doses of stimulating relationships with others in my field. In a more traditional setting, I can get that from co-workers, but by working out of my home I might feel cut off from that kind of stimulation.

Beyond Work: What other areas of your life hold the most promise for meeting your unmet needs?

> I can get involved in community service to fulfill some of my unmet needs—it would put me into touch with other professionals in my area. I can also turn to my personal relationships, and I can fill some of my need for intellectual stimulation on-line, by communicating with professionals on the Internet.

Confidence-Builders

Life Lessons: What 3 times have you felt good about yourself as a result of meeting your leftover needs beyond work?

> When I went out on my own in private practice, I addressed my need for collegiality by actively networking with other private practitioners by phone, e-mail, and in person. Later into my private practice, I also performed community service with colleagues by jointly offering pro bono workshops and presentations on career issues. And during my writing sabbatical, which was a particularly isolated period for me, I turned to my circle of close friends for intellectual stimulation and support.

Potential Outcomes: What's the worst thing that could happen if you tried to meet your leftover needs beyond work now? What's the best thing that could happen?

> The worst thing would be to find myself feeling lonely and isolated if I couldn't find the time or way to fill my need for collegiality. The best thing would be that, by having to take active steps to build or maintain contact with stimulating people, I end up with a wider and richer circle of colleagues than ever before.

Transformers

Talk-Over #1: How can you talk to yourself in a new way about your leftover needs that gives you a more flexible approach to directing your career?

> I can say: "I live surrounded by a wealth of experience and ideas with the people around me, and I can always reach out to them when I am unable to meet my needs all by myself."

Talk-Over #2: How can you talk to yourself in a new way about meeting your needs that gives you a more flexible approach to directing your career?

> I can say: "There are always new avenues for discovery and growth within my career—I just have to actively look for them when my current ideas aren't panning out the way I had hoped."

Conversation #11: Believing That Size Doesn't Matter

Explorers

Leftover Needs:

Beyond Work:

Confidence-Builders

Life Lessons:

Potential Outcomes:

Transformers

Talk-Over #1:

Talk-Over #2:

Conversation #12: Counting Three, Two, One, Lift-Off

Explorers

Space Travel: If someone asked you to describe in detail what you want to do next in your career, what would you say?

> I would want to use the core techniques I've used in my private practice to develop a pioneering self-help method that would integrate my three primary skills. This career would involve: writing a series of guided journals about self-development and lifestyle topics; leading spin-off seminars; and counseling clients on issues related to the topics.

Mission Control: What is it about this career that makes you feel passionate?

> I'm passionate about this career plan because it directly addresses my deepest needs: to help others improve the quality of their lives and to explore my talents to their fullest.

Confidence-Builders

Life Lessons: What 3 times have you felt good about yourself as a result of describing your next ideal career step and why you're passionate about it?

> When I discussed my goal of establishing a private practice to my colleagues, friends and family members, they supported me in my choice. Before I began teaching, my inner circle of supporters affirmed my gifts as a teacher. And whenever I spoke of my love of writing to the people around me, I appreciated receiving their advice and support as I looked for ways to integrate this skill into my overall career.

Potential Outcomes: What's the worst thing that could happen if you tried to develop your ideal career mission statement now? What's the best thing that could happen?

> The worst thing is that I might feel impatient about wanting to achieve all of my goals at once and faster than is realistic. The best thing would be that, by making concrete what I want and reminding myself of why I want it, I'll feel inspired to go after my career goals—no matter what.

Transformers

Talk-Over #1: How can you talk to yourself in a new way about space travel that gives you a more flexible approach to directing your career?

> I can say: "By articulating my next ideal career step, I can find the courage and resources to take it."

Talk-Over #2: How can you talk to yourself in a new way about mission control that gives you a more flexible approach to directing your career?

> I can say: "By remembering what drives me to take the next step, I can find the stamina to persevere when I hit a bump in the road."

Conversation #12: Counting Three, Two, One, Lift-Off

Explorers

Space Travel:

Mission Control:

Confidence-Builders

Life Lessons:

Potential Outcomes:

Transformers

Talk-Over #1:

Talk-Over #2:

STRUCTURE: Figuring It Out

3

The Conversations
   Considering alternative "when's" to work
   Answering "yes" to "got time?"
   Beating the clock mania
   Deciding who's the boss
   Counting how many jobs to have and to hold
   Making a family-friendly wish list
   Imagining a few of your favorite things
   Becoming a matchmaker
   Remodeling your environment
   Calculating dollars and sense
   Experimenting with shapes and sizes
   Designing a crazy quilt

Until recently, when, where, and how you worked has meant certain predictable things for most of us. It has meant spending a continuous block of hours at work; working away from home; answering to a manager; and following a single career path. But progressive organizations have amended these rules with flexible, unconventional arrangements. And many people have started exploring options beyond those found in the conventional world of work. Working moms, in particular, are paving the way for—and benefiting from—a wide variety of nontraditional arrangements as we attempt to juggle our parental responsibilities and the demands of our careers.

The Changing Nature of Work

Take the problem of inflexible hours. In the past, you usually worked a set number of hours, on a set schedule. Today there are lots of other arrangements, like flex-time and job-sharing, that allow workers to tailor their hours to the needs of their families. Employees are happier, because they have fewer conflicts between home and work, and employers are happier because absenteeism drops and job satisfaction among employees increases.

There's also been a big revolution in where you work. Sure, many jobs still require that you go to work in a location other than your home, but that's no longer the only choice available. Now there are lots of options, from telecommuting to home-based businesses, and these are becoming increasingly popular as more and more people search for ways to better integrate their lives.

And this brings us to another important change in the structure of work. In the past, having a job has generally meant working for somebody else. This has been a special problem for working moms, who often faced the dilemma of trying to handle at-home crises while keeping up with their work schedules. Many working moms today are choosing to become more independent—setting ourselves up as free agents and small-business owners.

These new options have also allowed many of us to fundamentally redefine what we do. With greater flexibility and autonomy, we're now free to combine several different skills or interests, inventing whole new career categories as we go along. Many working moms have realized that piecing together your work life from two or more different fields is a viable alternative—and one that can be immensely satisfying. As a working mom, then, your next challenge is to reassess how you structure your work life.

Finding Your Optimal Structure

In this part of the journal, you'll learn about alternative ways to work and consider which arrangements are best for you. You may even inspire yourself to make some changes, structuring your career to better manage your work and family lives. And, remember, my journal entries are here too. So if you get stuck on a question, you can check out my responses.

Conversation #13: Considering Alternative "When's" To Work

Explorers

Standard Time: What are the pros and cons of your currently scheduled working hours?

> Fortunately, right now my working hours are self-regulated. However, since I work on my own, there's nobody to cover for me if I've got work scheduled and have to face a sudden family crisis. When that happens, I have no choice but to cancel or reschedule everything, which causes some conflict.

Time Warps: What changes would you like to make in the way your work time is structured?

> I'd like to build a few half-days into my work-week, maybe picking up the slack by occasionally working on the weekend. I'd also like to be able to set aside a block of time in the summer for writing, reading, continuing education, and rejuvenating myself with my family. Maybe, someday, it would be fun to lead an intensive retreat for a small group of working moms.

Confidence-Builders

Life Lessons: What three times have you felt good about yourself as a result of when you worked?

> Switching from multi-week seminars to one-day workshops was good because it let me offer an experience in which the participants could acquire the tools they needed without having to make a long-term commitment. I was fortunate to be able to spend lots of time with my daughter during my writing sabbatical. It was also good to be able to cut down on late nights and tight deadlines that were becoming disruptive to my personal life.

Potential Outcomes: What's the worst thing that could happen if you tried to change when you worked? What's the best thing that could happen?

> The worst thing that could happen is that I'd be unable to maintain my effectiveness without a formal schedule. The best thing would be to have the luxury to take the time I needed for myself and my family—without the guilt.

Transformers

Talk-Over #1: How can you talk to yourself in a new way about your work's standard time that gives you a more flexible approach to structuring your career?

> I can say: "I can take the good things from my 9–5 experience into my home-based career, and still have the flexibility I need for myself and my family."

Talk-Over #2: How can you talk to yourself in a new way about time warps that gives you a more flexible approach to structuring your career?

> I can say: "Tempering structure with flexibility, while keeping a long-term view, is one of the most essential tools for balancing my home life with my home-based career."

Conversation #13: Considering Alternative "When's" To Work

Explorers

Standard Time:

Time Warps:

Confidence-Builders

Life Lessons:

Potential Outcomes:

Transformers

Talk-Over #1:

Talk-Over #2:

Conversation #14: Answering "Yes" To "Got Time?"

Explorers

What Means Most: How do you set your daily priorities? Why do you set priorities this way?

> Taking a moment at the start of the day to write a priority list is important. Giving a rank of importance to the things that need to be done lets me get the hard stuff done first when I'm fresh, which lets me do the more enjoyable stuff later when I'm tired—almost as a reward.

Every Little Thing: How would you characterize your self-imposed work standards as they currently exist? How well do you manage to live up to them?

> I tend to set unrealistic standards for myself, which just sets me up to be rough on myself if I'm unable to accomplish them as I had wished. Thankfully, I'm learning to be satisfied with my progress, and to value how messes, or accidents, often become innovations.

Confidence-Builders

Life Lessons: What three times have you felt good about yourself as a result of how you managed your priorities or standards?

> During my writing sabbatical I felt that I managed my priorities well. When I decided to break down the boundaries between the different aspects of my work, I reaped the benefit of a more fluid creative process. Finally, beginning to be able to look back and see what I have accomplished, instead of what I haven't, has been one of my greatest rewards.

Potential Outcomes: What's the worst thing that could happen if you realigned your priorities and adjusted your standards? What's the best thing that could happen?

> The worst thing is that I might feel like an underachiever if I start letting some things slide. But the best thing would be that I might finally get a chance to devote real time and energy to the things that matter most to me.

Transformers

Talk-Over #1: How can you talk to yourself in a new way about what means most that gives you a more flexible approach to structuring your career?

> I can say: "My 'to do' list is just for those things that have to be done within one day—it's ok to not be superwoman."

Talk-Over #2: How can you talk to yourself in a new way about your standards for every little thing that gives you a more flexible approach to structuring your career?

> I can say: "To do my best now is better than to try and do as well as I think I did yesterday—what's important is to be proud of my accomplishments."

Conversation #14: Answering "Yes" To "Got Time?"

Explorers

What Means Most:

Every Little Thing:

Confidence-Builders

Life Lessons:

Potential Outcomes:

Transformers

Talk-Over #1:

Talk-Over #2:

Conversation #15: Beating The Clock Mania

Explorers

Penning Yourself In: How often do you set aside time to pamper yourself? What, if anything, usually interferes with giving yourself some "pampering" time?

> Although I'd like to give myself a little pampering every day, it's usually the first thing off of my schedule when things fall behind—especially if it seems that someone else in the family needs me to pamper them more than I think I need it for myself.

Suspending Time: What everyday activities help rejuvenate your mind, body, and spirit? Why don't you pursue these nurturing activities more often?

> Listening to my favorite music, reading a good book, and doing a Pilate's workout are some of my favorite "do for me" things. Unfortunately, I don't do these things as often as I should, because when things get hectic I feel guilty for wanting to take any time for myself.

Confidence-Builders

Life Lessons: What three times have you felt good about yourself as a result of nurturing yourself in your favorite ways?

> Rewarding myself by taking a real vacation after completing a long, tense project was the best thing I could do for me. Picking up the phone to an old friend when the pressures got high renewed my self-esteem. And, finally, I made a conscious effort to find the time for a few of my favorite "do for me" things, and it gave me a tremendous boost that lasted for days afterward.

Potential Outcomes: What's the worst thing that could happen if you prioritized nurturing yourself now? What's the best thing that could happen?

> The worst thing that could happen is that I would feel selfish for spending time on myself instead of on my work or my family. The best thing would be that the boost in my spirits and my energy will be reflected in better efficiency at work and a greater ability to respond to my family's needs since my own have been taken care of.

Transformers

Talk-Over #1: How can you talk to yourself in a new way about penning yourself in that gives you a more flexible approach to structuring your career?

> I can say: "Just 15 minutes a day of 'just for me' time will make everything else that much easier to deal with."

Talk-Over #2: How can you talk to yourself in a new way about suspending time that gives you a more flexible approach to structuring your career?

> I can say: "No day is too busy that I should neglect myself. Self-neglect will only make things harder later."

Conversation #15: Beating The Clock Mania

Explorers

Penning Yourself In:

Suspending Time:

Confidence-Builders

Life Lessons:

Potential Outcomes:

Transformers

Talk-Over #1:

Talk-Over #2:

Conversation #16: Deciding Who's The Boss

Explorers

Becoming a Profiler: How would you describe your ideal boss?

> My ideal boss is realistic in her demands on my time, has a good sense of humor, is willing to take calculated risks, and is committed to lifelong learning and self-improvement. Frankly, my ideal boss is me—I'm happiest working under my own direction, and I like to think I possess those other characteristics as well.

Me or Somebody Else: Would you rather work for someone else or for yourself? Why?

> When I was less sure of myself, I didn't think I could be self-employed. Now that I have a stronger sense of direction, I prefer to have control over the nature and evolution of my work—and when, where, and how I do it.

Confidence-Builders

Life Lessons: What three times have you felt good about yourself as a result of your relationship with your boss, whether it was you or someone else?

> My boss—and mentor—when I was fresh out of college helped me grow professionally and personally. While I was attending graduate school, I had another boss who treated me as a colleague, which bolstered my sense of self. Now, I'm working for myself, and I'm proud of the way I've grown into my role, and have come to manage both the managerial and creative aspects of my work.

Potential Outcomes: What's the worst thing that could happen if you found or became your ideal boss now? What's the best thing that could happen?

> The worst thing that could happen if I went in search of the perfect boss now would be that I would end up disappointed. The best thing would be to find myself in a situation where my growth is enhanced and encouraged.

Transformers

Talk-Over #1: How can you talk to yourself in a new way about becoming a profiler that moves you toward a more flexible approach to structuring your career?

> I can say: "A good boss for me is one who reflects on who I am and how I work. I will strive to keep this quality in my professional life so that I can continue to grow."

Talk-Over #2: How can you talk to yourself in a new way about 'me or somebody else' that moves you toward a more flexible approach to structuring your career?

> I can say: "Who I work for is less important than the quality of my relationship with her—whether I'm my own boss or I work for someone else."

Conversation #16: Deciding Who's The Boss

Explorers

Becoming a Profiler:

Me or Somebody Else:

Confidence-Builders

Life Lessons:

Potential Outcomes:

Transformers

Talk-Over #1:

Talk-Over #2:

Conversation #17: Counting How Many Jobs To Have And To Hold

Explorers

Monogamy or Polygamy: How many different kinds of work do you want to do, in addition to being a parent? How much time would you like to devote to each of these jobs?

> I really don't want to have to choose between writing, teaching, and counseling—but I know I can't do all of these full time and still have energy left for my family. I'm still wrestling with exactly how much time to devote to each of these jobs, but right now I'm happiest if I spend most of my time writing.

For Better or For Worse: What is the basis of your commitment to the job or jobs you want to do?

> I'd like to find a way to balance all three of these jobs in one holistic career, because each one challenges a different set of skills, and all of them give me a great deal of satisfaction. Besides, they make a great combination—they all work together to strengthen my performance in each one.

Confidence-Builders

Life Lessons: What three times have you felt good about yourself as a result of how many jobs you've held at once?

> Allowing myself the opportunity to do just career counseling let me truly discover how I felt about it as a career path. When transitioning between the corporate world and a home-based career I was proud that I could maintain a stable income by taking temporary jobs, yet not lose sight of my main goal. Finally, since I've begun integrating writing with counseling and teaching, I feel charged up and confident as each one reinforces my performance in the other.

Potential Outcomes: What's the worst thing that could happen if you tried holding a different number of jobs or dividing your time among multiple jobs differently now? What's the best thing that could happen?

> The worst thing that could happen is that I feel over-extended and stressed out. The best thing would be that I'll have lots of different outlets for my skills, interests, and talents and will end up feeling more fulfilled.

Transformers

Talk-Over #1: How can you talk to yourself in a new way about monogamy or polygamy that gives you a more flexible approach to structuring your career?

> I can say: "Including a variety of different types of work will enrich both my professional and personal life."

Talk-Over #2: How can you talk to yourself in a new way about for better or for worse that gives you a more flexible approach to structuring your career?

> I can say: "Each of the jobs I want to do satisfies an important set of needs, and I can confirm my commitment to each of them by gradually integrating them into a complementary whole."

Conversation #17: Counting How Many Jobs To Have And To Hold

Explorers

Monogamy or Polygamy:

For Better or For Worse:

Confidence-Builders

Life Lessons:

Potential Outcomes:

Transformers

Talk-Over #1:

Talk-Over #2:

Conversation #18: Making A Family-Friendly Wish List

Explorers

Name Your Criteria: What's your wish list of policies and programs that would make a work environment family-friendly?

> My definition of a family-friendly work environment would include: flexible work hours, job sharing, and on-site or back-up child care, as well as paid maternity and paternity leave, child- and elder-care referral programs, the option of telecommuting, and counseling services.

Just Wishful Thinking: What's stopping you from getting your top three wish list items?

> I already have flexible work hours and would like to try job sharing my counseling or teaching duties, but I'm afraid of losing professional credibility. I've also found it difficult to come up with a reliable back-up arrangement for child care.

Confidence-Builders

Life Lessons: What three times have you felt good about yourself as a result of working in or fantasizing about working in a family-friendly work environment?

> I've had two university-based positions that provided a family-friendly work environment, and this made it possible for me to be much more responsive to my personal obligations. The same is true about a job I had at a progressive financial institution. In every case, I felt less stressed and more positive about my jobs because they respected my family needs.

Potential Outcomes: What's the worst thing that could happen if you pursued a family-friendly work environment now? What's the best thing that could happen?

> The worst thing that could happen is that I could lose work or credibility if I tried to institute some of my needs—particularly job-sharing. But if I could do it successfully, the best thing would be that my work life and home life would blend more smoothly.

Transformers

Talk-Over #1: How can you talk to yourself in a new way about your family-friendly criteria that gives you a more flexible approach to structuring your career?

> I can say: "I will consider all of my family-friendly work environment needs, but I accept that it may be realistic to meet only some of them at any one point in time—and that's ok."

Talk-Over #2: How can you talk to yourself in a new way about wishful thinking that gives you a more flexible approach to structuring your career?

> I can say: "The first step towards realizing a wish or a dream is to let myself imagine it coming true. The second step is to start talking to my supportive friends and colleagues about how to make it real."

Conversation #18: Making A Family-Friendly Wish List

Explorers

Name Your Criteria:

Just Wishful Thinking:

Confidence-Builders

Life Lessons:

Potential Outcomes:

Transformers

Talk-Over #1:

Talk-Over #2:

Conversation #19: Imagining A Few Of Your Favorite Things

Explorers

The Look: How would you describe your ideal physical surroundings at work?

My ideal work surroundings would be spacious and have lots of natural light. I'd like room enough to have an organized work area as well as a messy creative space, and a small conference table with a couple of comfortable chairs. Also, I want a door for privacy, a bookcase or two, lots of plants, and space to keep a few personal items, like photos and artwork, and a safe play area for my children.

The Feel: What's your idea of the best work-place dynamics?

When I'm writing I like a quiet, meditative space so I can get lost in my work. On the other hand, I like an energetic bustle of activity for seminar work, with people sharing ideas.

Confidence-Builders

Life Lessons: What three times have you felt good about yourself as a result of the look and feel of your work environment?

While I was never really happy with my physical work environment when I worked outside the home, I've felt productive and happy with my home offices, because they each largely reflected the look and feel of my personal style and made work seem inviting each time I entered them.

Potential Outcomes: What's the worst thing that could happen if you pursued a work environment that you loved the look and feel of now? What's the best thing that could happen?

The worst thing that could happen is that I could spend too much time decorating my space, rather than working in it. The best thing would be to create the ultimate sanctuary—a place that rejuvenates me and lets me both integrate and set boundries with my work and family lives.

Transformers

Talk-Over #1: How can you talk to yourself in a new way about the look of your work environment that gives you a more flexible approach to structuring your career?

I can say: "I deserve a comfortable, appealing workplace. It makes me much more willing to spend time there and is likely to increase my productivity."

Talk-Over #2: How can you talk to yourself in a new way about the feel of your work environment that gives you a more flexible approach to structuring your career?

I can say: "I deserve to work in an environment that fosters my creativity and encourages me to do the best job that I can."

Conversation #19: Imagining A Few Of Your Favorite Things

Explorers

The Look:

The Feel:

Confidence-Builders

Life Lessons:

Potential Outcomes:

Transformers

Talk-Over #1:

Talk-Over #2:

Conversation #20: Becoming A Matchmaker

Explorers

Selecting Prospects: Where can you find examples of work environments that both look and feel good to you?

I can look for examples in magazines and books and I can ask friends and colleagues for advice.

The Second Date: How can you distinguish between environments that make a good first impression only and that may genuinely be good for you?

I can talk with the people who work in these environments and spend some time visiting them there.

Confidence-Builders

Life Lessons: What three times have you felt good about yourself as a result of coming across examples of work environments that were right for you?

A friends elegant and distinctive home office sparked ideas for my own space that answered to my organizational needs. And another friend's office showed me how to integrate my family in my space—much needed since I work at home. More recently, I came across a magazine spread of budget-priced ideas for home-office renovations and found several that I felt sure I could use.

Potential Outcomes: What's the worst thing that could happen if you researched real life examples of your ideal work environment now? What's the best thing that could happen?

The worst thing is that I could fall in love with designs that are aesthetically satisfying but not practical enough to fit my needs. The best thing would be to find creative, cost-effective ways to get what I want.

Transformers

Talk-Over #1: How can you talk to yourself in a new way about scouting prospects that gives you a more flexible approach to structuring your workspace?

I can say: "It's important to look for examples of good and bad environments to continue to discover what I really need to work well."

Talk-Over #2: How can you talk to yourself in a new way about the second date that gives you a more flexible approach to structuring your career?

I can say: "What is truly important is that it not only looks right to me, but that it also feels right."

Conversation #20: Becoming A Matchmaker

Explorers

Scouting Prospects:

The Second Date:

Confidence-Builders

Life Lessons:

Potential Outcomes:

Transformers

Talk-Over #1:

Talk-Over #2:

Conversation #21: Remodeling Your Environment

Explorers

Assessing Your Needs: In what ways do the look and the feel of your current work environment match your ideal? In what ways do they fall short?

I've got the light I want, and my environment is comfortable—it's just too small and sometimes too noisy. I'd also like to personalize it a bit more.

Drawing a Blueprint: Which negatives can you change into positives and which negatives are beyond your control?

I can't change the size of my workspace, but I can look into creative storage ideas so that the available space is put to better use. I can also look for ways to reduce the noise that seeps into my space, and I can put a little more effort into making personal touches.

Confidence-Builders

Life Lessons: What three times have you felt good about yourself as a result of re-evaluating your work environment?

When I've remodeled my home office (I've done it three times now), I've felt good because I've managed to bring it a little closer to my ideal each time.

Potential Outcomes: What's the worst thing that could happen if you tried to make your current work environment fit your ideal one now? What's the best thing that could happen?

The worst thing that could happen is that I might disrupt my work flow while trying to remodel my space. The best thing would be to come up with a work environment that better suits my needs.

Transformers

Talk-Over #1: How can you talk to yourself in a new way about assessing your needs that gives you a more flexible approach to structuring your career?

I can say: "I will make a conscious effort to evaluate my current workspace to find changes that I can make to improve my work flow—and then make concrete plans to put these changes into place."

Talk-Over #2: How can you talk to yourself in a new way about drawing a blueprint that gives you a more flexible approach to structuring your career?

I can say: "There are always ways to overcome workspace problems—and that the time I spend on finding creative solutions is time well spent."

Conversation #21: Remodeling Your Environment

Explorers

Assessing Your Needs:

Drawing A Blueprint:

Confidence-Builders

Life Lessons:

Potential Outcomes:

Transformers

Talk-Over #1:

Talk-Over #2:

Conversation #22: Calculating Dollars And Sense

Explorers

The Real Bottom Line: What money issues are holding you back from changing your job or workplace?

> Right now I have to choose between remodeling my office and absorbing some possible initial loss of income if I change the direction of my work. I don't want to stretch my budget too tightly, because there's always the possibility of some unexpected expenses in any new business venture.

Balancing Your Values: At this point in your life, will changing your job or workplace help you to live more in synch with your values? If so, how?

> Modifying my job will help allow me to spend more time with my family and it will also let me explore more meaningful areas of my career. In the long run, it should also lead to a better and more stable income.

Confidence-Builders

Life Lessons: What three times have you felt good about yourself as a result of changing jobs or workplaces?

> Relocating from New York to Chicago because of a new job, made me feel that my work and my move both contributed to improving my quality of life. When I moved from the academic to the corporate sector, I felt good about moving into a situation where I could expand my skills and opportunities. And when I shifted the focus of a job I had in corporate human resources, I felt good about being able to spend more time on areas of my work that I enjoyed most.

Potential Outcomes: What's the worst thing that could happen if you changed jobs or workplaces now? What's the best thing that could happen?

> The worst thing would be to change jobs only to find that my new situation was no more rewarding than my old one was. The best thing would be to find a new work situation that better balances my personal and job-related needs.

Transformers

Talk-Over #1: How can you talk to yourself in a new way about the real bottom line that gives you a more flexible approach to structuring your career?

> I can say: "Making a temporary sacrifice financially for a better job or workplace is preferable to sticking with something that's not right just because it's more secure right now."

Talk-Over #2: How can you talk to yourself in a new way about balancing your values that gives you a more flexible approach to structuring your career?

> I can say: "It's important to keep a clear sense of my most important priorities, and use them as my principle criteria when judging a particular change or course of action."

Conversation #22: Calculating Dollars And Sense

Explorers

The Real Bottom Line:

Balancing Your Values:

Confidence-Builders

Life Lessons:

Potential Outcomes:

Transformers

Talk-Over #1:

Talk-Over #2:

Conversation #23: Experimenting With Shapes And Sizes

Explorers

Irregular Configurations: Have you ever considered drawing your work life from more than one source? What appeals to you or turns you off about such an arrangement?

> I've done it before and I'm considering doing it again. What I like is the freedom it gives me to truly create a multi-faceted, dream career. What turns me off is how easy it is to end up over-committing myself when I'm juggling several different jobs.

Starting Out Small: How could you downscale your ideal work to make it fit with your current home responsibilities?

> I could take it slowly—building my business at a comfortable pace that doesn't disrupt my family time, and I could take special care to limit the number of book projects, seminars, and clients I take on at any one time.

Confidence-Builders

Life Lessons: What three times have you felt good about yourself as a result of valuing the parts of your career as much as the whole?

> I felt good about myself when I took my sabbatical, and also while I attended both graduate school and my certificate program in the evening after working during the day. In each case, I gave myself permission to focus for awhile on one or another part of my career and explore it thoroughly.

Potential Outcomes: What's the worst thing that could happen if you downscaled or otherwise changed your approach to your career? What's the best thing that could happen?

> In the worst case scenario, downsizing my career or piecing together several different jobs could leave me feeling as if I'm slipping behind professionally. However, the best thing would be that I could find more flexibility and greater balance between my work life and my home life.

Transformers

Talk-Over #1: How can you talk to yourself in a new way about irregular configurations that gives you a more flexible approach to structuring your career?

> I can say: "Piecing together the current phase of my career from three part-time jobs is a respectable, creative solution to adapting my career to my lifestyle, which may also help me explore new options for the future."

Talk-Over #2: How can you talk to yourself in a new way about starting out small that gives you a more flexible approach to structuring your career?

> I can say: "If I need to slow down temporarily, it doesn't mean that I'll never reach my long-term goals. It just means that I'm respecting my limits. When my situation changes, I can always go back to a faster pace."

Conversation #23: Experimenting With Shapes And Sizes

Explorers

Irregular Configurations:

Starting Out Small:

Confidence-Builders

Life Lessons:

Potential Outcomes:

Transformers

Talk-Over #1:

Talk-Over #2:

Conversation #24: Designing A Crazy Quilt

Explorers

Arranging the Pieces: If you were to design the basic structure of your next ideal career step, what would it look like?

Ideally, I'd like to work half-days two or three days a week, with each of these days specifically dedicated to a single aspect of my career. During the summer I'd devote my time primarily to my family, cutting back on my career work.

The Quilting Bee: Write a make-believe newspaper ad for resources that might help you make this structure a reality.

"Working mom seeking other working mom entrepreneurs for advice about dealing with the practical and emotional aspects of redirecting a business. Willingness to share real-life perspectives and creative solutions required. Knowledge of software systems to manage tracking complex, expanding data needs a plus."

Confidence-Builders

Life Lessons: What three times have you felt good about yourself as a result of strategizing about the what, when, and how of your ideal career?

There are three career transitions during which I felt especially good about myself as a result of strategizing my ideal career: when I decided to go to graduate school, when I made a transition from higher education to the corporate world, and when I became self-employed.

Potential Outcomes: What's the worst thing that could happen if you tried to develop the structure of your ideal career now? What's the best thing that could happen?

The worst thing that could happen is that I get too caught up in the design details and make them too complex to work out. The best thing would be that I develop a flexible blueprint that I can refer to as I adapt my career to my lifestyle.

Transformers

Talk-Over #1: How can you talk to yourself in a new way about arranging the pieces that gives you a more flexible approach to structuring your career?

I can say: "By setting all the pieces out in front of me I will be better able to set realistic priorities about what needs to happen, and when."

Talk-Over #2: How can you talk to yourself in a new way about the quilting bee that gives you a more flexible approach to structuring your career?

I can say: "Writing out what kind of help I need to create an ideal career structure will remind me that it's possible and desirable to get good advice and support."

Conversation #24: Designing A Crazy Quilt

Explorers

Arranging the Pieces:

The Quilting Bee:

Confidence-Builders

Life Lessons:

Potential Outcomes:

Transformers

Talk-Over #1:

Talk-Over #2:

ADVANCEMENT: Moving Up, Down, Or Sideways

4

The Conversations
    Defining "being there"
    Scoring a goal
    Unlocking your resources vault
    Finding mentors who've "been there, done that"
    Working through your underground networks
    Noticing the gaps
    Learning your way
    Educating yourself
    Exploiting your soft skills
    Adding a personal touch
    Reviewing your working mom chronicles
    Rescuing yourself from a deserted island

Traditionally, getting ahead has involved scrambling up the organizational ladder as far and as fast as possible. It's also been a lonely enterprise—you were expected to advance solely through your own hard work. If you asked for help along the way, you weren't really "making it." So you stoically muddled through problems and focused on your short-term goals. Creativity was rarely rewarded—you were far more valued if you concentrated on developing specialized, technical skills. And, of course, you weren't supposed to rock the boat. You waited patiently for other people to rate your performance.

But these unwritten rules for career advancement don't apply in today's working world. The recent wave of alternative business, career, and life management options have rendered the old ways obsolete—and spawned a whole new set of philosophies about integrating work and home life. These philosophies have encouraged many people, particularly working moms, to design nontraditional strategies for achieving success on our terms.

Changing Measures of Advancement

In these new philosophies, the traditional symbols of advancement—money and status—are being challenged. People are coming to recognize that there are many other ways to measure success, including creative fulfillment, autonomy, and service, among others. And many workers, particularly women, are challenging the assumption that we have to work in isolation. Instead, we're turning to mentors, networking with colleagues, and forming partnerships that more realistically address our scheduling needs.

An even more profound change has occurred specifically in the way working moms approach their careers. Typically, we've focused only on short-term career goals, accepting the fact that employers simply weren't going to advance an employee who was likely to be torn between her responsibilities at home and her duties on the job. But today more and more working moms are learning to take a creative, flexible approach to our careers that allows us to keep our long-term goals on track.

Who's to Judge?

Finally, the traditional reward system is beginning to break down. Many working moms today are discovering that we don't need to wait for validation from our supervisor or manager. Instead, we're creating careers for ourselves in which we can provide our own performance feedback and rewards. We're becoming more proactive in creating work conditions that add meaning and satisfaction to our careers—and our lives.

All these changes start with one basic shift in philosophy: recognizing that there are many different ways to measure career growth and advancement beyond the traditional model. For working moms in particular, these nontraditional alternatives help us to redefine our concepts of success.

In this series of conversations, you'll explore new ways of using your personal and professional resources to improve your advancement strategies. In the process, you'll generate ideas for advancing your career in ways that are compatible with your lifestyle. And remember, if you feel confused about how to answer a question, you can use my journal notes as an example.

Conversation #25: Defining "Being There"

Explorers

Mapping It Out: What does success mean to you?

> Success means achieving my most significant goals—both big and little—in all aspects of my life.

Destination, Destination, Destination: How will you know when you've become successful?

> I'll just know—I'll feel good about myself as a result of my work and, more importantly, how I live my life.

Confidence-Builders

Life Lessons: What three times have you felt good about yourself as a result of how you defined and assessed your success?

> While transitioning into private practice, I defined my success by the small steps I took toward reaching this goal and felt good about myself while doing it. Receiving positive feedback about my various activities from others made me feel good about myself. And, finally, after the birth of my first child and my subsequent decision to downsize my private practice, I was proud of how I balanced my two roles—as a professional and as a parent.

Potential Outcomes: What's the worst thing that could happen if you made your definition of success more personal and more specific? What's the best thing that could happen?

> The worst thing that could happen is that I would be defeated by my fear of success. The best thing that could happen is that I'll learn how to more clearly define what I'm aiming for, so I'll know it when I've reached it.

Transformers

Talk-Over #1: How can you talk to yourself in a new way about mapping it out that gives you a more flexible approach to advancing your career?

> I can say: "Right now, success means staying true to my values: achieving creative fulfillment, providing service to others, maintaining balance between my career and my home life, and achieving financial stability."

Talk-Over #2: How can you talk to yourself in a new way about destination, destination, destination that gives you a more flexible approach to advancing your career?

> I can say: "My success comes when I consistently set and meet creatively challenging career and family goals and still maintain the balance I need between both those aspects of my life, and remember that financial success is only one part of a much bigger picture."

Conversation #25: Defining "Being There"

Explorers

Mapping It Out:

Destination, Destination, Destination:

Confidence-Builders

Life Lessons:

Potential Outcomes:

Transformers

Talk-Over #1:

Talk-Over #2:

Conversation #26: Scoring A Goal

Explorers

Hard Choices: What are your top three career goals?

> To make a unique contribution to the broad field of self-development; to redirect my business efforts as a counselor, writer, and teacher so that I'm working toward this goal in a more focused way; and to translate my activities into multi-media formats.

Living in the Present: What do you need to do next to achieve each of your goals?

> I need to clearly state what's distinctive about my counseling approach and identify how it relates to the idea of self-development. I need to work out how I want to combine my three activities so that they are most effectively integrated in my larger project, and where I need help—whether from people or multi-media resources—to do them effectively.

Confidence-Builders

Life Lessons: What three times have you felt good about yourself as a result of working towards your most important career goals?

> I felt that I was taking positive steps for future development when I pursued my master's degree in counseling. Moving to a private practice let me realize that I had the talent and the courage to make it as an independent professional. And I enjoy my book projects for the creative challenges they represent.

Potential Outcomes: What's the worst thing that could happen if you selected your top career goals and took small steps toward them now? What's the best thing that could happen?

> I'm afraid of failing to adequately clarify my goals and strategies for achieving them and stalling my career. But I hope to make real progress toward achieving my goals, while keeping my life balanced by staying realistic.

Transformers

Talk-Over #1: How can you talk to yourself in a new way about hard choices that gives you a more flexible approach to advancing your career?

> I can say: "It's important to remain flexible while not spreading myself too thin if I want to be truly effective—and satisfied—in my work."

Talk-Over #2: How can you talk to yourself in a new way about living in the present that gives you a more flexible approach to advancing your career?

> I can say: "I need to focus on one step at a time, and reward myself when I have achieved each one so that each part will feel just as important as the eventual whole I'm working towards."

Conversation #26: Scoring A Goal

Explorers

Hard Choices:

Living in the Present:

Confidence-Builders

Life Lessons:

Potential Outcomes:

Transformers

Talk-Over #1:

Talk-Over #2:

Conversation #27: Unlocking Your Resources Vault

Explorers

The Safe Deposit Box: What personal resources do you have enough of to help you advance in your career? What resources do you need more of to reach your goals?

At the moment, I have enough energy and emotional support to help me advance in my career. I need more time and money to help me reach my goals.

Growing Your Riches: How can you increase your personal resources?

Setting realistic and appropriate priorities will help me get the big things done on time, and also find ways to merge related tasks. Making sure I'm healthy and well-rested also makes me more productive. Finally, finding creative ways to reduce expenses will increase my financial resources.

Confidence-Builders

Life Lessons: What three times have you felt good about yourself as a result of tapping into your personal resources to advance your career?

I supplemented my emotional energy resources by getting into an informal support group of self-employed friends when I went into private practice. Rescheduling my work hours so that the tougher projects happened when my kids were taking naps helped balance things out. And it felt good when I chose to postpone a couple of less than essential purchases for the office.

Potential Outcomes: What's the worst thing that could happen if you tried to get the personal resources that you needed now? What's the best thing that could happen?

The worst thing that could happen is that I could still find myself needing more than I can get. The best thing that could happen is that I can come up with ways to advance my career faster, and with less effort and stress.

Transformers

Talk-Over #1: How can you talk to yourself in a new way about the safe deposit box that gives you a more flexible approach to advancing your career?

I can say: "The difference between wanting and needing is a big one. And by distinguishing between my wants and needs, I'll find creative ways to use the personal resources that I have to get ahead."

Talk-Over #2: How can you talk to yourself in a new way about growing your riches that gives you a more flexible approach to advancing your career?

I can say: "Saying things like: 'I need more time to make time,' or 'I need more money to make money' won't help. Learning how to better manage the resources I have available will."

Conversation #27: Unlocking Your Resources Vault

Explorers

The Safe Deposit Box:

Growing Your Riches:

Confidence-Builders

Life Lessons:

Potential Outcomes:

Transformers

Talk-Over #1:

Talk-Over #2:

Conversation #28: Finding Mentors Who've "Been There, Done That"

Explorers

Advising to Advance: What specific advancement issues are the hardest for you to deal with alone? How have you dealt with these?

I find it hard to objectively and constructively review my own performance on any level. Professionally speaking, I've turned to colleagues and asked them for their assessment, but I've also asked for advice from other self-employed moms.

Real Lifers: Who are some prospective working mom mentors for you? What are the pro's and con's of having each of these people as a mentor?

Although I have many mom mentors who are helpful in different ways, maybe the best person to turn to is my good friend Margeaux. We work in the same field and share similar philosophies of work and home life, and she's generally available.

Confidence-Builders

Life Lessons: What three times have you felt good about yourself as a result of seeking advice about advancing your career as a working mom?

When I started my private practice, I sought advice on directing it from more advanced practitioners. When my first child was born I turned to other working moms I knew for advice on how to set realistic goals and limits on my time and commitments. And when I discovered that I needed help managing the financial side of my business I talked to a lot of self-employed friends who had already dealt with this problem.

Potential Outcomes: What's the worst thing that could happen if you worked with a mentor to address your key working mom issues now? What's the best thing that could happen?

The worst thing that could happen is that I could not agree with the advice I get. The best thing would be to learn something new that can really help me and that I could find that I had built a support network that will help me gain more confidence in myself.

Transformers

Talk-Over #1: How can you talk to yourself in a new way about advising to advance that gives you a more flexible approach to advancing your career?

I can say: "I'm not alone in trying to create a new lifestyle—there are others who have traveled at least part of this road before me. Seeking advice from mentors will help me resolve challenging issues."

Talk-Over #2: How can you talk to yourself in a new way about real lifers that gives you a more flexible approach to advancing your career?

I can say: "I need to use many sources when seeking a mentor, and it's okay—and even helpful sometimes—to have more than one mentor at the same time as my needs change."

Conversation #28: Finding Mentors Who've "Been There, Done That"

Explorers

Advising to Advance:

Real Lifers:

Confidence-Builders

Life Lessons:

Potential Outcomes:

Transformers

Talk-Over #1:

Talk-Over #2:

Conversation #29: Working Through Your Underground Networks

Explorers

Timing It Right: When do you network (consult others to find out about career opportunities)?

> I network all of the time. I've learned that some of the best ideas come when you don't even know you're looking for them yet. And besides, it's fun and fascinating to learn what other people are doing and how they tell their stories.

Making Valuable Connections: How do you prefer to network? What stops you from networking?

> I try to stay open to networking opportunities all the time—both by letting them happen at work lunches, parties, supermarkets, kids' activities, the gym, and hobby classes, and by seeking them out at professional association events, through mentors, and through school alumni groups. However, sometimes I get too wrapped up in my work and then I tend to neglect to notice opportunities for networking.

Confidence-Builders

Life Lessons: What three times have you felt good about yourself as a result of networking to advance your career?

> I felt good about networking for client referrals when I was beginning to build my private practice, because it enabled me to grow a desirable, solid client base relatively quickly. Teaching opportunities have also come my way through networking, and I also discovered a fantastic consulting opportunity through networking.

Potential Outcomes: What's the worst thing that could happen if you committed yourself to strengthening and activating your network of contacts now? What's the best thing that could happen?

> The worst thing that could happen is that I spend too much time networking, because I enjoy it so much. The best thing would be to sharpen my networking skills so that networking becomes a powerful tool for furthering my career and bettering my lifestyle.

Transformers

Talk-Over #1: How can you talk to yourself in a new way about timing it right that gives you a more flexible approach to advancing your career?

> I can say: "It's important to network at least once a day, when I'm considering a way to adapt my career to my lifestyle even more."

Talk-Over #2: How can you talk to yourself in a new way about making valuable connections that gives you a more flexible approach to advancing your career?

> I can say: "Networking will help me to expand my career and lifestyle options. When I occasionally feel discomfort about asking for advice I will overcome it by offering help or advice in return, so that I don't feel so awkward."

Conversation #29: Working Through Your Underground Networks

Explorers

Timing It Right:

Making Valuable Connections:

Confidence-Builders

Life Lessons:

Potential Outcomes:

Transformers

Talk-Over #1:

Talk-Over #2:

Conversation #30: Noticing The Gaps

Explorers

Close-Ups and Panoramic Views: What missing skills, knowledge, or experience do you need to achieve your short-term and long-term career goals?

> I need to improve my market research skills so I can find out which self-improvement topics are most wanted by the public. I also need to get better at promoting my projects. Another area I need to learn more about is how I can use different media options more effectively.

Filling In on the Side: How do you plan to fill in your gaps?

> I've been reading up on current trends in my field and I've been learning more about marketing on my own as well. Talking with people who have had professional experience in many of the areas I need to learn more about has also helped. I also intend to take some courses when time and money are available.

Confidence-Builders

Life Lessons: What three times have you felt good about yourself as a result of developing your skills to advance your career?

> It felt good to know that I was expanding my knowledge to benefit my career when I completed my certificate program in adult career development and planning. It also felt good to "learn by doing" when I started developing and teaching workshops and seminars. When it comes to my writing—every project I take on teaches me more, which helps me in my overall career development.

Potential Outcomes: What's the worst thing that could happen if you identified and planned to fill in your skill, knowledge, or experience gaps now? What's the best thing that could happen?

> The worst thing would be to find that I'm spending so much time filling in my gaps that my day-to-day business suffers. The best thing would be to find that even my current business gains from the new skills I'm using, and that my advance preparation makes my transition to a new career focus much smoother.

Transformers

Talk-Over #1: How can you talk to yourself in a new way about close-up and panoramic views that gives you a more flexible approach to advancing your career?

> I can say: "I need to consistently take stock of what specific skills, knowledge, or experience I need to reach my short-term goals and my long-term goals."

Talk-Over #2: How can you talk to yourself in a new way about filling in on the side that gives you a more flexible approach to advancing your career?

> I can say: "Everything I'm doing now provides me with opportunities to expand or refine my skills—and I need to keep myself open to recognizing new learning experiences in everything I do."

Conversation #30: Noticing The Gaps

Explorers

Close-Ups and Panoramic Views:

Filling In on the Side:

Confidence-Builders

Life Lessons:

Potential Outcomes:

Transformers

Talk-Over #1:

Talk-Over #2:

Conversation #31: Learning Your Way

Explorers

The Easy Way: What is your preferred ways to learn new things?

> I prefer learning new things by reading books and researching topics on the Internet first, then by discussing the issues with others. Then I apply what I've learned to real projects.

The Hard Way: How would you describe your least favorite ways of learning?

> I don't enjoy plowing through dry, jargon-filled textbooks or sitting through dull lectures.

Confidence-Builders

Life Lessons: What three times have you felt good about yourself as a result of learning new things in a way that was comfortable for you?

> Developing and leading a stress-management workshop during graduate school, completing a case study project in my certificate program, and facilitating the redesign of a company's management practices were all hands-on, rewarding experiences.

Potential Outcomes: What's the worst thing that could happen if you used your learning strengths to advance your career now? What's the best thing that could happen?

> The worst thing would be to find that I've ignored a valuable learning possibility simply because it wasn't presented in a style that I enjoy. The best thing would be to discover that, by seeking out opportunities that suit my learning style, I pick up the skills and information I need faster and reinforce my commitment to continuing to learn and grow.

Transformers

Talk-Over #1: How can you talk to yourself in a new way about the easy way that gives you a more flexible approach to advancing your career?

> I can say: "There are many different ways to learn new skills and information and I need to seek such options out whenever possible."

Talk-Over #2: How can you talk to yourself in a new way about the hard way that gives you a more flexible approach to advancing your career?

> I can say: "If I'm stuck in an undesirable learning situation—like a giant lecture class—I can think up ways to make it more positive."

Conversation #31: Learning Your Way

Explorers

The Easy Way:

The Hard Way:

Confidence-Builders

Life Lessons:

Potential Outcomes:

Transformers

Talk-Over #1:

Talk-Over #2:

Conversation #32: Educating Yourself

Explorers

Your Motivations: How could continuing your education help you advance your career?

> I already have the general credentials I need to make the career transition I plan, but there are particular skills I need to develop or improve so I'll still want to take some specialized courses. Plus, participating in courses will give me a chance to network with new people, while surrounding myself with others who are interested in the same topics will keep me enthusiastic and will spark new ideas.

Exploring Your Options: How can you get the particular skills and knowledge you need to advance your career?

> Right now I don't have the time or financial resources to sign up for courses at the university, but I can do independent research at the library and on-line and I can get involved in on-line chat groups, workshops, and seminars.

Confidence-Builders

Life Lessons: What three times have you felt good about yourself as a result of educating yourself to advance your career?

> I felt good about myself after earning my graduate degree, completing my certificate program, and reading extensively about learning styles to advance my career. Each of these experiences gave me greater confidence in my abilities, sharpened my skills, and brought me closer to achieving my professional goals.

Potential Outcomes: What's the worst thing that could happen if you committed yourself to continuing your education now? What's the best thing that could happen?

> The worst thing would be to find that continuing my education takes time away from the nitty-gritty tasks related to developing my business. The best thing would be to find that the time I've spent continuing my education is well rewarded as I become more skilled and the quality of my work improves.

Transformers

Talk-Over #1: How can you talk to yourself in a new way about your motivations that gives you a more flexible approach to advancing your career?

> I can say: "It's important to continue my education so that I can stay on the cutting edge of new research in my fields, share ideas with others, and earn the respect of my peers and clients."

Talk-Over #2: How can you talk to yourself in a new way about exploring your options that gives you a more flexible approach to advancing your career?

> I can say: "I can make a list of the many different continuing education options available to me that are convenient, affordable, and geared to my needs."

Conversation #32: Educating Yourself

Explorers

Your Motivations:

Exploring Your Options:

Confidence-Builders

Life Lessons:

Potential Outcomes:

Transformers

Talk-Over #1:

Talk-Over #2:

Conversation #33: Exploiting Your Soft Skills

Explorers

Soft Stuff: What interpersonal or "people" skills do you have that could help you progress in your career?

> I'm a good listener, and I've developed skills in mediating and facilitating discussions. I believe I'm good at developing and maintaining relationships. And I'm good at giving advice without getting preachy or bossy.

Naming the Sources: Through what specific experiences in your life have you developed each of these skills?

> Many of my interpersonal skills—like listening and maintaining relationships—developed over the course of my whole life, and have been refined especially through my roles as wife, mother, and friend. For some I've had formal training—in school and on the job.

Confidence-Builders

Life Lessons: What three times have you felt good about yourself as a result of using your interpersonal skills to advance your career?

> Effectively advising students about career issues and teaching career workshops were both great experiences, because they showed me that I had important talents for my dream career. And, all of my interpersonal skills enabled me to attract a strong client base in my private practice.

Potential Outcomes: What's the worst thing that could happen if you focused on developing your most career-relevant interpersonal skills now? What's the best thing that could happen?

> The worst thing that could happen is that I focus too much on my soft skills at the expense of my hard skills. The best thing, since soft skills are especially key in my fields, I improve them greatly and, in turn, advance my career farther faster.

Transformers

Talk-Over #1: How can you talk to yourself in a new way about your soft stuff that gives you a more flexible approach to advancing your career?

> I can say: "My abilities to listen actively to others' problems; facilitate a discussion; and maintain strong relationships with others are invaluable assets to my career growth. They complement my technical skills and are what distinguishes me as a balanced, progressive professional."

Talk-Over #2: How can you talk to yourself in a new way about naming the sources that gives you a more flexible approach to advancing your career?

> I can say: "All sources for developing soft skills—including non-paid ones like volunteer work, hobbies, and parenting—are valuable. I'm proud when I participate in such activities and my growth in these arenas is intimately connected with my career advancement."

Conversation #33: Exploiting Your Soft Skills

Explorers

Soft Stuff:

Naming the Sources:

Confidence-Builders

Life Lessons:

Potential Outcomes:

Transformers

Talk-Over #1:

Talk-Over #2:

Conversation #34: Adding A Personal Touch

Explorers

Fingerprinting Yourself: What is unique about your approach to work that distinguishes you from others in your field?

> I've developed a unique, self-directed, action-oriented approach to career counseling and self-improvement. I also believe that I'm unusually willing to explore new ideas and learn new skills. And my client-centered, enthusiastic attitude also helps me to stand out in my field.

Standout Ideas: How can you use these distinctive qualities to advance your career?

> I can find ways to consolidate my techniques into a core method that can help others solve their key problems. I can use my openness to new ideas and skills to help me keep growing in my profession. And I can use my attitude to attract new clients and writing projects.

Confidence-Builders

Life Lessons: What three times have you felt good about yourself as a result of adding a personal touch to your work?

> I have felt good about personalizing my services for each client's needs and styles because it shows me that I really listen to them. Writing with an action-oriented, self-directed approach has let me share "recipes" of success with my readers so that they could "cook" for themselves. And it has felt good to know that my commitment and enthusiasm is appreciated by those who attend my workshops and seminars.

Potential Outcomes: What's the worst thing that could happen if you directed your personal touches to advance your career now? What's the best thing that could happen?

> The worst thing would be to discover that people weren't receptive to what I have to offer. The best thing would be to find that my unique skills are truly appreciated by others.

Transformers

Talk-Over #1: How can you talk to yourself in a new way about fingerprinting yourself that gives you a more flexible approach to advancing your career?

> I can say: "Others may share my unique qualities in general, but it's the personal spin I put on them that makes me special."

Talk-Over #2: How can you talk to yourself in a new way about standout ideas that gives you a more flexible approach to advancing your career?

> I can say: "I should apply my unique qualities in as many situations as possible. For example, I can distinguish myself as particularly client-centered by sending clients hand-written thank you notes, rather than preprinted ones that I just sign."

Conversation #34: Adding A Personal Touch

Explorers

Fingerprinting Yourself:

Standout Ideas:

Confidence-Builders

Life Lessons:

Potential Outcomes:

Transformers

Talk-Over #1:

Talk-Over #2:

Conversation #35: Reviewing Your Working Mom Chronicles

Explorers

Pacing Your Progress: When do you review your performance as a working mom?

I usually spend a little time at night before I go to sleep reviewing how I'm doing. If I'm feeling particularly stressed out by family demands, I'll catch myself judging myself about how I'm juggling my career and family life. More constructively, I'll assess how I'm doing when I'm talking with other working moms who share some of my problems.

Looking Both Ways: What record do you have of these working mom reviews? How do you typically review yourself as a working mom?

I try to keep a record of how I'm doing in a lot of ways. I keep a journal, which records my day-to-day self-assessment. But I also keep letters of praise, thank-you notes, ticket stubs from special events, and other such mementos of those times when I've felt that my efforts have been appreciated.

Confidence-Builders

Life Lessons: What three times have you felt good about yourself as a result of reviewing your performance as a working mom?

On Mother's Day when my family told me how proud they are of me, I felt that perhaps I was doing okay after all. The last time I was feeling down about myself professionally, I looked through my "brag file"—a collection of letters of praise for my work—and felt a lot better. On my last birthday I read through my last year's journal entries and realized how much I've grown over that time—it felt good to see how far I've come.

Potential Outcomes: What's the worst thing that could happen if you committed yourself to regularly reviewing your performance as a working mom now? What's the best thing that could happen?

I could end up obsessing about every little thing I do, and focusing only on the negatives. That would be devastating. On the other hand, I could end up with a clearer view of myself and find ways to improve my performance without beating up on myself.

Transformers

Talk-Over #1: How can you talk to yourself in a new way about pacing your progress that gives you a more flexible approach to advancing your career?

I can say: "It's only productive to review my performance when I can be objective and constructive—not when I'm already feeling stressed out or inadequate."

Talk-Over #2: How can you talk to yourself in a new way about looking both ways that gives you a more flexible approach to advancing your career?

I can say: "I'm a strong person who always tries to do my best in both my career and family life. If I'm having trouble, I'll remember my past successes and use what I've learned to turn difficult situations around."

Conversation #35: Reviewing Your Working Mom Chronicles

Explorers

Pacing Your Progress:

Looking Both Ways:

Confidence-Builders

Life Lessons:

Potential Outcomes:

Transformers

Talk-Over #1:

Talk-Over #2:

Conversation #36: Rescuing Yourself From A Deserted Island

Explorers

The Strategic Approach: What strategies are you using to advance your career? How do you choose which ones to use at any given time?

> I use networking, continuing my education, and working with a mentor to advance my career. I'm pretty good about matching my strategy to my specific goal, but sometimes I'll just do whatever comes to mind.

Zigging and Zagging: What kinds of work and family issues tend to sabotage your strategic plans? What kinds of personal issues tend to sabotage your strategic plans?

> Sometimes I lose sight of my strategic plans because I'm too busy just trying to cope with the details. Sometimes an unexpected event throws my planning out of whack. Also, I sometimes sabotage myself by procrastinating.

Confidence-Builders

Life Lessons: What three times have you felt good about yourself as a result using a strategic approach to advancing your career?

> Deciding to pursue my certificate to supplement my master's degree and professional experience is still paying off for me. Consulting with one of my mentors about how to adapt my career to my lifestyle after the birth of my first child brought me good advice and reassurance. And taking a strategic approach to pursuing my writing projects made them successful.

Potential Outcomes: What's the worst thing that could happen if you focused on taking one, small step to advance your career now? What's the best thing that could happen?

> The worst thing would be to get bogged down in the planning stage and never actually act on my strategies. The best thing would be to find that this first step provides me with the momentum I need to see my plan through to the end.

Transformers

Talk-Over #1: How can you talk to yourself in a new way about the strategic approach that gives you a more flexible approach to advancing your career?

> I can say: "I must keep my strategic planning simple and do-able. I need to be methodical in my planning and carefully assess my plan's usefulness each step of the way."

Talk-Over #2: How can you talk to yourself in a new way about zigging and zagging that gives you a more flexible approach to advancing your career?

> I can say: "Listing the obstacles that stand in the way of developing and executing a strategic plan, and dividing them into the things I can easily change and the ones over which I have less control, let me map out realistic strategies for overcoming those obstacles."

Conversation #36: Rescuing Yourself From A Deserted Island

Explorers

The Strategic Approach:

Zigging and Zagging:

Confidence-Builders

Life Lessons:

Potential Outcomes:

Transformers

Talk-Over #1:

Talk-Over #2:

SECURITY: Changing Just Enough 5

The Conversations
  Profiling your risk-ability
  Opening your mind
  Believing it when you see it
  Walking the talk
  Sharpening your technology edge
  Increasing your visibility
  Becoming a trend-weaver
  Reinventing yourself
  Bouncing off the past
  Designing a multi-faceted career
  Kissing and telling why you're changing
  Cutting the chase scene

In the past, job security has been characterized by a steady paycheck, benefits, and long-term job stability. It's been awarded by paternalistic employers to employees who have demonstrated both an unconditional loyalty to working for their organization and a don't-make-waves attitude at work. But the world of work has changed. Long-term job security has been compromised by down-sizing, layoffs, and restructuring. Workers have responded to these changes in the work world by making some changes of their own.

A hallmark of the new millennium has been this attitude shift, especially among working moms. We're no longer seeking security as a "gift" from our employers. Instead, we're exploring new ways to manage our careers—ways that allow us to manage our responsibilities without jeopardizing the financial security that many of our families count on us to help provide.

This shift has redefined the concept of security. No longer does it automatically mean minimizing your risk-taking. No longer do working moms have to adopt a tunnel-vision approach to our career development, plodding along traditional paths. Now, the world of work necessitates taking a few risks. The most effective way to maintain your working value is to actively seek out alternatives—change—by looking for everyday needs that you can address with your skills, and by keeping on top of the latest developments in your field.

The Challenge of Living with Change

Consistent with the old-style approach, it has been considered impulsive—and even foolish—for working moms to follow trends about when, where, and how to work. But those days are over. We now know that by incorporating selected trends, you can make it easier to adapt your career to your lifestyle. You no longer have to be content with stifling your own changing needs and preferences, as well as hiding your failures, in order to preserve your professional reputation. Instead, it has become vital to reinvent yourself from time to time. And by sharing your career experiences with others—even the unsuccessful ones—you can earn their respect and increase your likelihood of making successful future changes.

Above all, staying open to change does not necessarily mean living with insecurity. As a working mom, your challenge concerning change, then, is to reconsider how you view and manage the relationship between risk-taking and security. And that's what this collection of conversations is all about.

Break Down Your Barriers

In the next journal entries, you'll explore the kinds of change that you can make to develop a more rewarding approach to your career. You'll gain an understanding of how you can surpass the conventional limitations of the workplace while still achieving security in your work life.

Your goal during these journal entries is to embrace change. Throughout these next several pages, you'll be asked to rethink your current approach to change, determining how much risk is necessary for you to keep up with change. And, once again, you're welcome to read my reflections whenever you feel puzzled about how to deal with the issues.

Conversation #37: Profiling Your Risk-Ability

Explorers

Your Risk Threshold: In navigating your career, and making plans to adopt your career to your lifestyle, would you consider yourself to be a low risk-taker, moderate risk-taker, or high risk-taker?

> Generally, I've been a moderate to high risk-taker as I've evolved my career. I'm approaching my current crossroads with a combination of the two: I'm taking an unconventional approach to my work (high risk), while maintaining a moderate pace (medium risk) so that I can keep all aspects of my life well-balanced.

Making Change: What specific risks do you need to take now to adapt your career to your lifestyle in terms of where, when, and/or how you work? What are your current fears about taking these risks?

> I need to a take a risk by attempting to create a fairly consistent work schedule and pace while still maintaining as much flexibility as possible. Another risk is trying to conduct my expanding venture in limited space. A third risk is adopting new technologies with which to conduct my work. My fear is in making the change itself: starting something new is always scarier than actually doing the new things once I've taken the first steps.

Confidence-Builders

Life Lessons: What three times have you felt good about yourself as a result of risking change to make your career more secure?

> Relocating—from New York to Chicago—felt really good once I'd made the change. So did shifting from a conventional counseling practice to a more specialized niche. Making a break from my normal routine to take a writing sabbatical was also risky—but it's really paying off and will make my career more secure in the end.

Potential Outcomes: What's the worst thing that could happen if you faced your fears and took a calculated career risk now? What's the best thing that could happen?

> The worst thing would be to discover that a change I make won't fit with my lifestyle needs after all. The best thing that could happen is that I'll find an even better work and lifestyle fit that truly suits my needs, priorities, and desires.

Transformers

Talk-Over #1: How can you talk to yourself in a new way about your risk threshold that gives you a more flexible approach to securing your career?

> I can say: "The key to my career growth, and my career security, is to be willing to take risks as I see the need to adapt."

Talk-Over #2: How can you talk to yourself in a new way about making change that gives you a more flexible approach to securing your career?

> I can say: "I need only take risks that are essential to adapting my career to my lifestyle. I don't need to make change just for the sake of change."

Conversation #37: Profiling Your Risk-Ability

Explorers

Your Risk Threshold:

Making Change:

Confidence-Builders

Life Lessons:

Potential Outcomes:

Transformers

Talk-Over #1:

Talk-Over #2:

Conversation #38: Opening Your Mind

Explorers

Looking, Listening, and Connecting: What specific ways do you stay aware of options for change in your career?

Through networking; attending lectures on relevant topics; reading broadly about social, economic, political, and cultural trends; and talking with others to get a feel for their careers.

Checking Out Possibilities: How far are you willing to go to explore your options?

I'm willing to keep a journal of my thoughts and feelings as I contemplate making changes. I'm also willing to interview for jobs; draft business plans; and experiment with new ways to work.

Confidence-Builders

Life Lessons: What three times have you felt good about yourself as a result of becoming aware of or exploring your career options?

Exploring new (to me) applications of my professional training felt good. So did my exploration of the growing educational software development market to see how my talents might be used in that area. And receiving an invitation to become professionally involved with a progressive start-up company made me feel confident and optimistic about my career options in high tech ventures.

Potential Outcomes: What's the worst thing that could happen if you became more actively aware and willing to explore your career options now? What's the best thing that could happen?

I'm afraid that exploring my options will make me feel the need to vastly change everything that I have done in the past. The best thing that could happen is to discover that the new alternatives are really a natural extension of what came before, and that my new direction makes me happier than ever.

Transformers

Talk-Over #1: How can you talk to yourself in a new way about looking, listening, and connecting that gives you a more flexible approach to securing your career?

I can say: "Simple ways for me to expand my awareness of my career options are all around me—all I need to do is stay open to them by talking to colleagues, to surfing the Internet, reading, and just plain thinking creatively."

Talk-Over #2: How can you talk to yourself in a new way about checking out possibilities that gives you a more flexible approach to securing your career?

I can say: "Exploring career options can give me hope, keep me excited about my future, and provide me with the security of knowing that there are many ways that I can modify my career to fit my lifestyle needs."

Conversation #38: Opening Your Mind

Explorers

Looking, Listening, and Connecting:

Checking Out Possibilities:

Confidence-Builders

Life Lessons:

Potential Outcomes:

Transformers

Talk-Over #1:

Talk-Over #2:

Conversation #39: Believing It When You See It

Explorers

Common Lifestyle Needs: What are some services that you and others around you need on a regular basis related to caring for selves, families, homes, and businesses?

> Hmmm—it's a pretty long list: stress management, child care, elder care, pet care-taking, budgeting, meal preparation, clothes and gift shopping, home decorating, party planning, computer support, organizing, and career and life balance counseling.

Initiative Blockers: What's stopping you from pursing a career opportunity that meets a common lifestyle need?

> I need more confirmation that my idea for reinventing my business will work.

Confidence-Builders

Life Lessons: What three times have you felt good about yourself as a result of using your skills, knowledge, and experience to meet others' lifestyle needs?

> When I focused my writing projects on career and life balance issues; when I counseled clients who prioritized lifestyle issues in their career planning process; and when I advised other moms about their home-based career options, I felt good about using my gifts to help others meet their lifestyle needs.

Potential Outcomes: What's the worst thing that could happen if you used your gifts to provide a needed lifestyle service now? What's the best thing that could happen?

> The worst thing that could happen is that I burn out from letting myself focus on just one lifestyle issue all of the time. The best thing that could happen is that I provide a needed lifestyle service that addresses a variety of issues so that I'm stimulated and don't feel boxed in.

Transformers

Talk-Over #1: How can you talk to yourself in a new way about common needs that gives you a more flexible approach to securing your career?

> I can say: "I can expand and confirm my list of lifestyle needs that are common enough to form the basis of a good business venture."

Talk-Over #2: How can you talk to yourself in a new way about initiative blockers that gives you a more flexible approach to securing your career?

> I can say: "I can transform a common lifestyle need into a service business by exploring the best fit between my interests, talents, values, and personality style and the many alternative businesses related to the need."

Conversation #39: Believing It When You See It

Explorers

Common Lifestyle Needs:

Initiative Blockers:

Confidence-Builders

Life Lessons:

Potential Outcomes:

Transformers

Talk-Over #1:

Talk-Over #2:

Conversation #40: Walking The Talk

Explorers

Learning the Lingo: How do you keep on top of the latest jargon and ideas behind it in your field?

> I can stay current by reading magazines, journals, and newspapers, talking with colleagues, and through on-line resources like newsletters and message boards.

Showing and Telling: How can you integrate the latest developments in your field into your career? How do you let others know that you're on the cutting edge?

> I can integrate the latest developments by testing them out in model scenarios to see if they pan out. I can let others know I'm on the cutting edge by mentioning these developments when promoting my business to others.

Confidence-Builders

Life Lessons: What three times have you felt good about yourself as a result of keeping current with new developments in your field?

> When I first began offering long-distance counseling services; when I started writing about the value of self-managing your career; and when I began teaching topical workshops, I felt good because I was offering cutting edge services to my clients, readers, and students.

Potential Outcomes: What's the worst thing that could happen if you immersed yourself in the most recent innovations in your field and demonstrated your knowledge to others now? What's the best thing that could happen?

> The worst thing would be to be perceived as being too trendy by those whose approval matters most to me. The best thing that could happen is that I grow as a professional and offer the best grounded, yet innovative, services to others in every aspect of my work.

Transformers

Talk-Over #1: How can you talk to yourself in a new way about learning the lingo that gives you a more flexible approach to securing your career?

> I can say: "Jargon and buzzwords come and go quickly, but it's important for me to be aware of them so that I maintain my reputation as a well-informed, competitive professional."

Talk-Over #2: How can you talk to yourself in a new way about showing and telling that gives you a more flexible approach to securing your career?

> I can say: "I can experiment with applying new developments in my field to current or new projects. When I find something that works for me, I can show and discuss these improvements with my colleagues and clients."

Conversation #40: Walking The Talk

Explorers

Learning the Lingo:

Showing and Telling:

Confidence-Builders

Life Lessons:

Potential Outcomes:

Transformers

Talk-Over #1:

Talk-Over #2:

Conversation #41: Sharpening Your Technology Edge

Explorers

High Tech Advances: What technology do you like using to facilitate your communication? How do you figure out what technology is best for you?

> I like using my computer, a cordless phone, and a fax machine. I choose the technologies I'll use by reading articles and reviews; talking to other people who already use them; trying them out for myself to see how comfortable they feel; and by comparison shopping.

The Double Edge: How could using more technology benefit your career and make it more adaptable to your lifestyle? How could using more technology complicate your life?

> Using more technology could enable me to access and consolidate more information; streamline my bookkeeping; and work from multiple locations. Using more technology could complicate my life by making it too easy for people to reach me when I'm not supposed to be working.

Confidence-Builders

Life Lessons: What three times have you felt good about yourself as a result of using the technology in your career?

> Learning to use the Internet to keep on top of the latest trends and incorporating both computer and fax communications in my business made me feel more professional and confident. Installing a separate business phone in my home office felt good too, because it let me separate my work and personal phone lives, enriching both of them.

Potential Outcomes: What's the worst thing that could happen if you assessed your use of technology now? What's the best thing that could happen?

> The worst thing is that I need to take time away from current projects to research and update the technology that I use. The best thing would be that I learn to simplify my operations and free up my time for more meaningful work and life pursuits.

Transformers

Talk-Over #1: How can you talk to yourself in a new way about high tech advances that gives you a more flexible approach to securing your career?

> I can say: "Technology is a valuable tool as long as I choose what feels most comfortable and most fits my needs."

Talk-Over #2: How can you talk to yourself in a new way about the double edge that gives you a more flexible approach to securing your career?

> I can say: "The advantages of technology outweigh the disadvantages if I set clear boundaries about my work and personal time, and only buy the technology that I really need."

Conversation #41: Sharpening Your Technology Edge

Explorers

High Tech Advances:

The Double Edge:

Confidence-Builders

Life Lessons:

Potential Outcomes:

Transformers

Talk-Over #1:

Talk-Over #2:

Conversation #42: Increasing Your Visibility

Explorers

Highlighting Your Assets: How and when do you showcase your abilities and achievements? What's stopping you from doing it more?

> I mainly showcase my abilities and achievements through my work itself and in interviews to promote my books. I stop myself from doing it more when I get too bogged down in the day-to-day details of my work and become isolated from the larger world.

A View from the Top: How do you determine what abilities and achievements to focus on promoting?

> I usually end up promoting my most recent projects. I also try to tune in to what my colleagues and mentors consider to be important.

Confidence-Builders

Life Lessons: What three times have you felt good about yourself as a result of promoting your abilities and achievements?

> It felt good when I satisfied the participants in my workshops. When I first got into consulting and found that I quickly gained the respect of my colleagues I felt validated professionally. And going through the (multi-media) process of promoting my third book was exciting and empowering.

Potential Outcomes: What's the worst thing that could happen if you increased your visibility now? What's the best thing that could happen?

> The worst thing is feeling too much like a "show off" for promoting myself. The best thing is to discover that people really want to hear about what I have to offer and that promotion will help my business grow and prosper.

Transformers

Talk-Over #1: How can you talk to yourself in a new way about highlighting your assets that gives you a more flexible approach to securing your career?

> I can say: "Self-promotion can be done in many different ways—and it's in my best interest to discover, and pursue, the ways that best suit my style, my personality, and my business."

Talk-Over #2: How can you talk to yourself in a new way about a view from the top that gives you a more flexible approach to securing your career?

> I can say: "I have important, worthwhile gifts to share with others—but they'll never know it unless I tell them."

Conversation #42: Increasing Your Visibility

Explorers

Highlighting Your Assets:

A View from the Top:

Confidence-Builders

Life Lessons:

Potential Outcomes:

Transformers

Talk-Over #1:

Talk-Over #2:

Conversation #43: Becoming A Trend-Weaver

Explorers

Weaving Perceptions: What trends in the world of work about when, where, and how people work could you weave into your career that make you appear to be progressive?

> Some ideas I have are: offering selected early morning, evening, or other appointment hours to clients who work alternative hours; providing on-site services at clients' workplaces; and arranging on-line conferences.

Entwining Patterns: How could becoming a trend-weaver make it easier for you to adapt your career to your lifestyle? What challenges does becoming a trend-weaver pose?

> By becoming a trend-weaver I can adjust my work hours to match my lifestyle preferences; increase my autonomy, client base, and flexibility; and save myself travel time and expenses. It could hurt if it requires adding work hours at inconvenient times; requires more travel than I want; or costs too much by requiring that I invest in too much high-tech equipment.

Confidence-Builders

Life Lessons: What three times have you felt good about yourself as a result of weaving work world trends into your career?

> Switching to private practice to accommodate my lifestyle was a positive move. Offering multiple locations and high tech accessibility to my services. And restructuring my fee schedules to that clients could select from retainer, package, and hourly rates was another work trend that I used successfully.

Potential Outcomes: What's the worst thing that could happen if you experimented with when, where or how you worked to keep up with a trend now? What's the best thing that could happen?

> The worst thing that could happen is getting caught up in investigating too many trends at once—I need to be selective and try out only those that are appropriate to my specific needs. The best thing that could happen is that I make myself more accessible and secure in my career.

Transformers

Talk-Over #1: How can you talk to yourself in a new way about weaving perceptions that gives you a more flexible approach to securing your career?

> I can say: "I will select trends that make sense for both my field and my clients. As I pioneer such trends, I will attract new clients and increase the satisfaction of my current ones."

Talk-Over #2: How can you talk to yourself in a new way about entwining patterns that gives you a more flexible approach to securing your career?

> I can say: "By incorporating trends that work for both my clients and myself, I can secure my career without compromising my lifestyle needs."

Conversation #43: Becoming A Trend-Weaver

Explorers

Weaving Perceptions:

Entwining Patterns:

Confidence-Builders

Life Lessons:

Potential Outcomes:

Transformers

Talk-Over #1:

Talk-Over #2:

Conversation #44: Reinventing Yourself

Explorers

Creative Tensions: How do you become aware of changes in the interests and skills that you'd most prefer to use in your career?

> It becomes obvious when I begin to spend more time on some types of projects and start letting others slide. When I catch myself complaining about my work, I'm probably registering a desire to try something different. Also, when the normal demands of my work begins to really stress me out, it's a sure sign that my interests and skills are no longer being fully addressed.

Cycles of Loss and Renewal: How do you grieve loss and celebrate renewal—the normal sensations that accompany change of any sort—as you reinvent yourself in your work?

> In some cases I might turn to the reassurance of mundane tasks like reorganizing my files. In others I might try writing a reassuring letter to my "pre-change" self. If time and resources allow it, I might take a vacation to mark the shift in my life or simply buy something new for my work wardrobe that reflects my new self.

Confidence-Builders

Life Lessons: What three times have you felt good about yourself as a result of adapting your career to your changing preferences?

> Pursuing a career in career counseling; integrating counseling with writing and teaching; and taking a sabbatical to focus on my writing showed me that I could adapt my career to my changing needs.

Potential Outcomes: What's the worst thing that could happen if you reinvented yourself now? What's the best thing that could happen?

> The worst thing would be that I end up with a sense of loss instead of a sense of growth. The best thing that could happen is that I feel ready for my new, evolved self.

Transformers

Talk-Over #1: How can you talk to yourself in a new way about creative tensions that gives you a more flexible approach to securing your career?

> I can say: "I will pay attention to how my needs change and learn to be more pro-active by keeping a journal to track my feelings on how my career is meshing with my personal needs."

Talk-Over #2: How can you talk to yourself in a new way about cycles of loss and renewal that gives you a more flexible approach to securing your career?

> I can say: "Healthy growth requires a pause every once in awhile to acknowledge the sadness as well as the exhilaration that can accompany making a change."

Conversation #44: Reinventing Yourself

Explorers

Creative Tensions:

Cycles of Loss and Renewal:

Confidence-Builders

Life Lessons:

Potential Outcomes:

Transformers

Talk-Over #1:

Talk-Over #2:

Conversation #45: Bouncing Off The Past

Explorers

Springboard Skills: What related skills do I have that I can use in my new career direction? What unrelated skills do I have that I can use as leverage to launch my new career?

My counseling, teaching, and writing skills, as well as my business development skills, are all directly transferable to my spin-off career. I can't think of any unrelated skills right now that will help me.

Past-Future Connections: Who do I have access to who could help me make my next career move? Which of my employers might be a good place to rebound my career?

A few of my former teachers, several of my colleagues, and all of my current mentors could help me make my next career move. One former employer might be a good source of contacts for launching my seminars, and another supervisor can put me in touch with a few people experienced in on-line services.

Confidence-Builders

Life Lessons: What three times have you felt good about yourself as a result of using past skills or connections to further your career?

When I applied my academic skills—researching, writing, and interviewing—to my first career development-related job, I felt really good about myself. Also, taking my writing skills to the next stage by authoring my first book felt good, as did using my research skills to investigate new career options.

Potential Outcomes: What's the worst thing that could happen if you strategically used your skills and connections to make a career change now? What's the best thing that could happen?

The worst thing would be to discover that my contacts can't help me after all—or simply don't want to try. The best thing that could happen is that I end up launching a new phase of my career with key skills and support systems in place as a bridge between the old and new.

Transformers

Talk-Over #1: How can you talk to yourself in a new way about springboard skills that gives you a more flexible approach to securing your career?

I can say: "If I review my whole career history, I can find key skills that are in demand in the world of work and that I can apply to my next career move."

Talk-Over #2: How can you talk to yourself in a new way about past-future connections that gives you a more flexible approach to securing your career?

I can say: "It's always worth getting in touch with past work contacts; as long as I'm respectful about it, the people I contact will feel flattered that I'm seeking their advice."

Conversation #45: Bouncing Off The Past

Explorers

Springboard Skills:

Past-Future Connections:

Confidence-Builders

Life Lessons:

Potential Outcomes:

Transformers

Talk-Over #1:

Talk-Over #2:

Conversation #46: Designing A Multi-Faceted Career

Explorers

Temporary Solutions: How could you piece together your career to help you make a transition from an old one to a new one?

> I could do my current work part-time and start my new business on the side, so that the transition isn't too abrupt.

Permanent Arrangements: How could you re-arrange your current career or create a new one that involves multiple components? What percentage of your work time would you ideally want to devote to each component?

> Rather than putting the lion's share of time into teaching and counseling, which take me away from home more than I would like right now, I can increase the time I devote to writing, which I can do from my home office. This increases my availability to my children without requiring me to bring my career to a halt. And later on, I can renegotiate the mix as my needs change.

Confidence-Builders

Life Lessons: What three times have you felt good about yourself as a result of fantasizing about or actually piecing together your career?

> Working full-time by day in a permanent position while pursuing my studies at night let me use the insights from both worlds to enrich my overall career and academic life. Adding teaching to my counseling career was another great combination. And when I began writing while still actively counseling and conducting seminars was a really fruitful endeavor that enhanced all three pursuits.

Potential Outcomes: What's the worst thing that could happen if you designed either a temporary or permanent multi-faceted career now? What's the best thing that could happen?

> The worst thing would be to misjudge how much time I can devote to each aspect of my career—I could end up burned out and exhausted. The best thing would be to find that this combination approach exercises all my talents, keeping me excited and challenged in all aspects of my career and personal life.

Transformers

Talk-Over #1: How can you talk to yourself in a new way about temporary solutions that gives you a more flexible approach to securing your career?

> I can say: "It's okay to be honest about my limitations in order to protect myself from burning out, and glean, instead, hope and renewed energy for the task at hand."

Talk-Over #2: How can you talk to yourself in a new way about permanent arrangements that gives you a more flexible approach to securing your career?

> I can say: "By creating a multi-faceted career on a long-term basis I can best answer my needs for diversity, flexibility, and security."

Conversation #46: Designing A Multi-Faceted Career

Explorers

Temporary Solutions:

Permanent Arrangements:

Confidence-Builders

Life Lessons:

Potential Outcomes:

Transformers

Talk-Over #1:

Talk-Over #2:

Conversation #47: Kissing And Telling Why You're Changing

Explorers

Leaking the Story: When is the best time to reveal your plans for change to key others? What are some of the ways that would be most comfortable and appropriate to share this information?

> If I'm planning a change that will affect my household's economic security, I talk to my husband as soon as I've worked out just what I hope to do—after all, he's probably got some helpful suggestions. I don't broadcast my plans for change to colleagues until I've got a pretty good plan worked out, however, and I don't spread the word to clients until I'm ready to put that plan into action. If I'm looking for advice on making the change, I do it face-to-face or by telephone. If I'm announcing the change, I may use e-mail or regular letters.

Emphasizing the Future: How can you make sure that you're broadcasting the news of any career changes without being perceived as defensive, insecure, or incompetent?

> I can highlight my vision for my career move; tune others into the key points of the change story; and put a positive spin on my transitional activities.

Confidence-Builders

Life Lessons: What three times have you felt good about yourself as a result of when and how you've told others about your career changes?

> When I considered becoming a career counselor, I told family and friends in person during the brainstorming phase and it was great to get their supportive input. When I specialized my practice, I informed my colleagues and acquaintances by phone and e-mail before I implemented the plan so people had time to adjust. When I took a writing sabbatical, I let people know in person, by phone, and by e-mail, just after I decided to make the move for sure.

Potential Outcomes: What's the worst thing that could happen if you planned when and how to deliver career change news now? What's the best thing that could happen?

> The worst thing would be to make an error in timing and delivery—that could jeopardize the integrity and success of my change. The best thing would be to handle it smoothly so my colleagues and others will support me and will continue to see me as a credible professional.

Transformers

Talk-Over #1: How can you talk to yourself in a new way about leaking the story that gives you a more flexible approach to securing your career?

> I can say: "Different people need to know about my career plans at different phases of the process, and by controlling the announcement I can help ensure my success."

Talk-Over #2: How can you talk to yourself in a new way about emphasizing the future that gives you a more flexible approach to securing your career?

> I can say: "It's important to emphasize to others where I want to go with my career so that my changes won't disrupt my own career or place unfair burdens on them."

Conversation #47: Kissing And Telling Why You're Changing

Explorers

Leaking the Story:

Emphasizing the Future:

Confidence-Builders

Life Lessons:

Potential Outcomes:

Transformers

Talk-Over #1:

Talk-Over #2:

Conversation #48: Cutting The Chase Scene

Explorers

Checking the Rearview Mirror: What have you learned from your past career changes about what worked, what didn't, and why?

> I learned that my ability to stay open to opportunities, research the potential fit between options and my needs, use a combination of my gut and my head to make decisions, and fully devote myself to the change all affect whether things work or not.

Taking the Scenic Route: How can you increase your chances for making successful changes in your career?

> I can check out my options and select the ones that seem right for who I am at the time without dwelling on the others.

Confidence-Builders

Life Lessons: What three times have you felt good about yourself as a result of learning from past mistakes and successes and applying this knowledge to future career changes?

> Striking out on my own as a counselor, leading career workshops, and becoming a full-time writer are three changes that involved taking some serious risks. But by doing them I discovered that I was able to handle the changes, which bolstered my self-confidence and reaffirmed my sense of my own adaptability.

Potential Outcomes: What's the worst thing that could happen if you became more thoughtful and selective about your career changes now? What's the best thing that could happen?

> The worst thing would be to become paralyzed by overanalyzing each change before I make it. The best thing would be to develop better skills and greater confidence as a decision-maker and doer.

Transformers

Talk-Over #1: How can you talk to yourself in a new way about checking the rearview mirror that gives you a more flexible approach to securing your career?

> I can say: "Two things are crucial to making better career changes as time goes on: truly listening to myself and to the advice of others, and learning to let go of my fear of making a mistake."

Talk-Over #2: How can you talk to yourself in a new way about taking the scenic route that gives you a more flexible approach to securing your career?

> I can say: "If I thoroughly research my options for change, take a reasonable amount of time to reflect on those options, and accept my limits, I'll become a savvy at making career change strategies."

Conversation #48: Cutting The Chase Scene

Explorers

Checking the Rearview Mirror:

Taking the Scenic Route:

Confidence-Builders

Life Lessons:

Potential Outcomes:

Transformers

Talk-Over #1:

Talk-Over #2:

BALANCE: Losing It No More

6

The Conversations
- Going to extremes
- Sorting your style laundry
- Climbing the family tree
- Banning guilt and overcompensation
- Taking creative shortcuts
- Make needs meet
- Accommodating life happenings
- Mixing and matching your standards
- Saying "No" to impossible demands
- Streamlining your home work
- Cloning yourself
- Springing the comparison trap

As generations of working moms share their experiences, it's clear that one problem stands out as difficult: how to achieve a good balance in life while fulfilling both career and family responsibilities. Commonsense advice suggests that the way to manage this is to avoid going to extremes; keeping to the old, established ways of doing things; avoiding shortcuts; and keeping your own expectations low while trying to meet the expectations of others. But while these strategies can lead to achieving balance of a sort, they are very limiting. It's no wonder, then, that contemporary working moms are replacing them with more flexible, self-interested tactics.

Not all of these alternative strategies have been helpful, however. For example, working moms often slip into the overcompensation trap—trying to do too much, at work and at home—and exhausting ourselves. And, all the while, we compare ourselves to other working moms, convinced that we're just not doing enough. Or we go to the opposite extreme—dreaming too small—accepting less success at work and at home than is possible. And we convince ourselves that this is the price we have to pay for continuing to work once we have children.

But many working moms today are reversing this formula. We're dreaming big, and making it work by taking things a little more slowly and helping each other to accept our inevitable shortcomings. We're taking a close look at the traditional ways of organizing our work and home lives, and discovering new methods that better meet our needs.

Goodbye Superwoman!

Through the 1970s and 1980s, many working moms got caught up in the "superwoman" myth. They felt that they had to be the perfect career professional at work while still single-handedly dealing with all the demands of running a household and caring for their families. Taking a shortcut, asking for help, or revising standards were all unthinkable—you had to do it all. The result? A lot of over-tired, over-stressed, and unhappy working moms.

Today, the superwoman myth is gradually being replaced in the media and among real working moms by an acceptance that you can't do it all—and you shouldn't have to. We're beginning to recognize that we have the right to define the best balance in our lives, and to go after that balance on our own terms. But to do this, we have to re-evaluate just what kind of balance works best in our own lives—and then we have to give ourselves permission to create that balance, even if it means doing things differently from the way our own moms, or friends, or colleagues, do them.

Developing Your Own Balancing Act

In the twelve guided conversations that follow, you'll be challenged to explore the current balance—or lack of it—in your life. You'll look at the kinds of assumptions you've made up to now about the way you allocate your resources, and you'll discover that there are changes you can make that will help you achieve a more balanced, satisfying life at home and on the job. You'll ultimately discover that you aren't bound by the traditional definitions of how to be a mother, or a worker, and learn that by adjusting your approach to each of these roles you can achieve the balance that is most comfortable for you.

As you embark on this next set of conversations, you'll learn new ways to accommodate your best interests and priorities. You'll find out where you need to set limits, and develop a flexible approach to achieving a sense of balance between competing demands at work and at home. If you need a little help to get you started, feel free to read my answers to the questions—maybe you'll find a little inspiration in the way that I responded.

Conversation #49: Going To Extremes

Explorers

Dreaming Big: How would you describe, in as much detail as possible, an ultimate career dream of yours?

> To make a significant contribution to the field of self-development by taking the action-oriented techniques I've used in my private practice and integrating them into a self-directed method. I would then teach this method to others through a series of guided journals, live and on-line seminars, and in-person and on-line consulting.

Stepping It Out: What steps do you plan to take to make this dream a reality? What's your ideal timeline for taking each step?

> The first step is to write a guided journal to anchor the series, ideally within a year. Then I need to develop and lead a seminar based on this journal, as well as establish and promote a linked private practice, within six months of publication.

Confidence-Builders

Life Lessons: What three times have you felt good about yourself as a result of planning for your big career dreams?

> When I planned for going to graduate school in counseling, getting my first self-initiated book published, and taught my first career issues workshop, I felt energized and in the groove of doing what I was meant to be doing to go after my big career dreams.

Potential Outcomes: What's the worst thing that could happen if you allowed yourself to both dream big and take small steps towards that dream now? What's the best thing that could happen?

> To give in to my fear of failing and never achieve my dreams would be the worst thing possible. To learn to set motivating goals, and manageable ways to go after them, would be the best thing because it would give me the confidence, energy, and hope to persevere during the tough times.

Transformers

Talk-Over #1: How can you talk to yourself in a new way about dreaming big that gives you a more flexible approach to achieving balance in your life?

> I can say: "The bigger I dream, the more likely it is that I will aim to fulfill my authentic purpose in life."

Talk-Over #2: How can you talk to yourself in a new way about stepping it out that gives you a more flexible approach to achieving balance in your life?

> I can say: "Breaking down what it takes to achieve my ultimate career dream into the smallest steps possible is the best way to approach making it a reality."

Conversation #49: Going To Extremes

Explorers

Dream Big:

Step It Out:

Confidence-Builders

Life Lessons:

Potential Outcomes:

Transformers

Talk-Over #1:

Talk-Over #2:

Conversation #50: Sorting Your Style Laundry

Explorers

The Clean Pile: What are you doing at work and at home that's helping you to maintain balance in your life?

> When adhered to, having organizing systems for every space in the house, communication systems that allow me to separate my work life and home life effectively, placing a priority on family rituals, remaining flexible in my work hours, and having back-up childcare systems have all helped me keep my ducks in a row.

The Dirty Pile: What are you doing that's throwing you off balance and needs a fresh approach?

> Communications tend to go haywire when allowed to go unchecked, which tends to end up with things not getting the proper follow-through, and often with overlapped commitments. This leads to family rituals getting scattered, and takes away all flexibility—as well as undermining the effectiveness of any back-up plans I have set up.

Confidence-Builders

Life Lessons: What three times have you felt good about yourself as a result of separating what's contributing from what's detracting from balance in your life?

> Allowing myself to not have to be on all the time, such as screening calls, lowering my standards about having things neat all the time, and adjusting work around family time (rather than the other way around) made me feel good about achieving a better balance in my life.

Potential Outcomes: What's the worst thing that could happen if you sorted your clean and dirty laundry now? What's the best thing that could happen?

> The worst thing that could happen is that I feel daunted by getting others to adapt to my desired changes. The best thing that could happen is that my family, colleagues, and I all benefit from the new arrangements.

Transformers

Talk-Over #1: How can you talk to yourself in a new way about the clean pile that gives you a more flexible approach to achieving balance in your life?

> I can say: "Applying my natural skills to achieve a balance between my work and home life will make things much easier than if I try to re-invent the wheel every time there's a snag."

Talk-Over #2: How can you talk to yourself in a new way about the dirty pile that gives you a more flexible approach to achieving balance in your life?

> I can say: "Just because something worked yesterday, I need to be open to the fact that as things around me change, I need to change with them, and be open to the idea that change can be good and healthy."

Conversation #50: Sorting Your Style Laundry

Explorers

The Clean Pile:

The Dirty Pile:

Confidence-Builders

Life Lessons:

Potential Outcomes:

Transformers

Talk-Over #1:

Talk-Over #2:

Conversation #51: Climbing The Family Tree

Explorers

Exploring the Roots: How does your family define the work-family balance? What, if any, inconsistencies do you notice between what they say and what they do, and how does it affect your idea of what the balance should be?

I remember my family pretty much saying that family came first and that during the work week, the men had to do whatever it took to keep their job and support the family, which of course meant that they couldn't always be there. They handled that by sharing the balance between the women and the men. While I respected and loved—and felt loved by—my parents, I still wish I had had more time with my dad, and that my mom had been able to devote more time to her needs.

Sitting in the Branches: How do you define work-family balance? How does your definition differ from the definitions of balance you learned growing up?

My definition is a flexible, ever-evolving arrangement through which both sides of my life get nurtured. It's similar to what I learned as a child, because my parents taught me to recognize my limitations, but it's different in that my definition involves integrating the two.

Confidence-Builders

Life Lessons: What three times have you felt good about yourself as a result of achieving work-family balance?

When I began working exclusively from home, downsized my private practice, and took a writing sabbatical are three times that I achieved work-family balance in ways that felt satisfying.

Potential Outcomes: What's the worst thing that could happen if you used your self-knowledge to refine the way you define work-family balance now? What's the best thing that could happen?

The worst thing that could happen is that needing to constantly be flexible may make me feel that a work-family balance is always just out of my reach. The best thing that could happen is that I come to accept that striving for balance, and doing the best I can, is more than good enough.

Transformers

Talk-Over #1: How can you talk to yourself in a new way about exploring the roots that gives you a more flexible approach to achieving balance in your life?

I can say: "My parents taught me that there are always options. The mixed messages that I may have received taught me that what my parents do by example often sends a more powerful message than what they say."

Talk-Over #2: How can you talk to yourself in a new way about sitting in the branches that gives you a more flexible approach to achieving balance in your life?

I can say: "I will make what I say more consistent with what I do by discussing this issue with my family, admitting when I blow it, and planning with them for times when the balance needs to tip more to one side or the other."

Conversation #51: Climbing The Family Tree

Explorers

Exploring the Roots:

Sitting in the Branches:

Confidence-Builders

Life Lessons:

Potential Outcomes:

Transformers

Talk-Over #1:

Talk-Over #2:

Conversation #52: Banning Guilt And Overcompensation

Explorers

Guilt Triggers: In what specific situations related to balancing your work and family lives do you most often feel guilty about not being able to do enough?

> Having work impose on family time, as well as family time impose on getting work done are both tough situations, because they both make me feel as if I'm not able to do enough.

Reacting vs. Acting: When you react impulsively to your guilt, what do you do to try to compensate? When you act reasonably in response to making a difficult choice, what do you do to restore balance in your life?

> I often try to compensate for my guilt by apologizing excessively and by taking on more than my fair share of the next big work or home project. It's much healthier when I alternate my work and home commitments; deciding which events are most important; and offering to help out colleagues, family, and friends when they need work or home-related coverage.

Confidence-Builders

Life Lessons: What three times have you felt good about yourself as a result of banning guilt and overcompensation?

> I felt good about banning guilt and overcompensation when I limited the number of clients I took on during a busy season; when I did interviews to promote my books during early morning "rush" hour; and when I scheduled project deadlines with lots of extra time built in just in case unexpected things came up along the way.

Potential Outcomes: What's the worst thing that could happen if you banned guilt and overcompensation as much as possible now? What's the best thing that could happen?

> The worst thing would be to catch myself feeling guilty and overcompensating, and then berate myself for slipping up. The best thing would be that I free up lots of energy to enjoy my work and family lives, feel more comfortable about being an imperfect, but real, person, and set this example for my children.

Transformers

Talk-Over #1: How can you talk to yourself in a new way about guilt triggers that gives you a more flexible approach to achieving balance in your life?

> I can say: "I'm always going to have overlapping commitments to my work and family lives. Becoming more aware of my most frequent and painful types of situations can help me practice dealing with them better."

Talk-Over #2: How can you talk to yourself in a new way about reacting versus acting that gives you a more flexible approach to achieving balance in your life?

> I can say: "When I feel guilty I need to close my eyes for a moment, listen to some relaxing music, and/or take a deep breath before doing anything to address the guilt. That way I can regain my balance instead of automatically overcompensating for my guilt."

Conversation #52: Banning Guilt And Overcompensation

Explorers

Guilt Triggers:

Reacting vs. Acting:

Confidence-Builders

Life Lessons:

Potential Outcomes:

Transformers

Talk-Over #1:

Talk-Over #2:

Conversation #53: Taking Creative Shortcuts

Explorers

Mapping Your Routes: What work and family tasks do you tend to do in advance, keep up with as you go, or simultaneously to save time?

> I need to prepare for the next day before I go to bed—for myself and my children—by making lunches and laying out clothes. There are other things that help too: such as buying holiday gifts in advance, keeping a running shopping list, and doing dishes and laundry as well as printing reports and filing at the same time.

Navigating the Back Roads: How do you make work and family tasks easier to accomplish by cooperating with others?

> I barter items, like clothes, or services like career counseling, for goods and services that I need.

Confidence-Builders

Life Lessons: What three times have you felt good about yourself as a result of taking creative shortcuts?

> When I used the Internet to order and send a bunch of birthday and holiday presents; got in the habit of putting my financial transactions into my computer records daily; and took five minute bites out of one important long-term work and one home project until they both got done, I felt good about how these creative shortcuts kept me from feeling overwhelmed.

Potential Outcomes: What's the worst thing that could happen if you took more shortcuts about when and how you accomplished your work and family tasks now? What's the best thing that could happen?

> The worst thing that could happen is I try to do too much at once and end up making more work for myself overall. The best thing that could happen is that I free up more time every day for fun, meaningful work and family activities.

Transformers

Talk-Over #1: How can you talk to yourself in a new way about mapping your routes that gives you a more flexible approach to achieving balance in your life?

> I can say: "Doing more tasks in advance and at the same time will make me more efficient, and help to balance my work and family lives, without becoming over-extended and exhausted."

Talk-Over #2: How can you talk to yourself in a new way about navigating the back roads that gives you a more flexible approach to achieving balance in your life?

> I can say: "Bartering or rotating common tasks with my friends can be a one-time or trial arrangement as well as a long-standing one. I can try it out and see if it works for me."

Conversation #53: Taking Creative Shortcuts

Explorers

Mapping Your Routes:

Navigating the Back Roads:

Confidence-Builders

Life Lessons:

Potential Outcomes:

Transformers

Talk-Over #1:

Talk-Over #2:

Conversation #54: Making Needs Meet

Explorers

Ideal and Real Time: What is your ideal balance between your work and family time each week? What is your typical real balance between your work and family time each week?

My ideal balance is working about 20 hours a week. My typical real balance varies from 20 to many more hours a week.

Family Expectations: What are your family's expectations of your work-family balance? How do you deal with these expectations, especially when they don't match your ideal scenario or when they're not realistic at this point for you?

My family's expectations of my work-family balance basically match mine in terms of hours. What gets tricky is when my work hours need to be longer than desired for brief periods of time to get a project going or completed. Then I usually try to discuss the best way for us as a family to manage these times.

Confidence-Builders

Life Lessons: What three times have you felt good about yourself as a result of managing your and your family's work-family balance needs?

When I tried out variations on how to downsize my practice, worked out how to get through book promotion crunch times, and took a writing sabbatical, I felt good about meeting both my family's and my needs.

Potential Outcomes: What's the worst thing that could happen if you tried to improve your work-family balance to meet everyone's needs now? What's the best thing that could happen?

The worst thing that could happen is that I feel as if there's nothing more I can do. The best thing that could happen would be that I have shown how much I care and that it helps us bond as a family even more, supporting everyone's individual needs better.

Transformers

Talk-Over #1: How can you talk to yourself in a new way about ideal and real time that gives you a more flexible approach to achieving balance in your life?

I can say: "When necessary, I can make my real work-family balance match my ideal one better by adjusting when, where, and how I work."

Talk-Over #2: How can you talk to yourself in a new way about family expectations that gives you a more flexible approach to achieving balance in your life?

I can say: "I need to do what I can to meet my family's expectations, but also have the courage to discuss things that seem to be unrealistic expectations with them calmly and try to find other ways to meet their needs, as long as we do it together."

Conversation #54: Making Needs Meet

Explorers

Ideal and Real Time:

Family Expectations:

Confidence-Builders

Life Lessons:

Potential Outcomes:

Transformers

Talk-Over #1:

Talk-Over #2:

Conversation #55: Accommodating Life Happenings

Explorers

Extenuating Circumstances: Under what personal or family conditions can you imagine choosing to change your career life in any way?

> Burnout, a special interest project, or a family crisis.

Homing In on Alternatives: How could you adapt your career to accommodate these circumstances?

> I could reduce my work load, redirect my career to focus on a single area, or take time off.

Confidence-Builders

Life Lessons: What three times have you felt good about yourself as a result of making a change in your career to adapt it to an unusual personal or family circumstance?

> When I downsized my private practice and modified my other activities after the birth of my first child, took a writing sabbatical when my first child was one, and took a break from working altogether for a few months after the birth of my second child, I felt good about how I made changes in my career to adapt it to personal and family circumstances.

Potential Outcomes: What's the worst thing that could happen if you considered your career options for dealing with such circumstances now? What's the best thing that could happen?

> The worst thing that could happen is that I have trouble coming up with acceptable scenarios because they don't seem real ahead of time. The best thing that could happen is that I feel more prepared with possibilities and can deal better if I need to act on them.

Transformers

Talk-Over #1: How can you talk to yourself in a new way about extenuating circumstances that gives you a more flexible approach to achieving balance in your life?

> I can say: "I need to take comfort in remembering that my work-family balance will shift over time between being more focused on my work and being more focused on my personal life to various degrees. Being a working mom is just inherently a messy role that's always in flux."

Talk-Over #2: How can you talk to yourself in a new way about homing in on alternatives that gives you a more flexible approach to achieving balance in your life?

> I can say: "When I need to accommodate my career to difficult circumstances, I can explore many different options to figure out which one best meets my needs."

Conversation #55: Accommodating Life Happenings

Explorers

Extenuating Circumstances:

Homing In on Alternatives:

Confidence-Builders

Life Lessons:

Potential Outcomes:

Transformers

Talk-Over #1:

Talk-Over #2:

Conversation #56: Mixing And Matching Your Standards

Explorers

Letting Go: In what areas of your work and family lives are you willing to lower your standards when necessary to maintain balance in your life?

Right now, but not always, setting tight deadlines and exceeding others' expectations.

Holding On: In what areas of your work and family lives are your standards particularly high and inflexible?

Right now, but not always, maintaining orderliness and being accessible.

Confidence-Builders

Life Lessons: What three times have you felt good about yourself as a result of keeping some standards high and others lower than usual when necessary?

Learning to lower my standards for exceeding others' expectations during my writing sabbatical; learning to let go of compulsive orderliness during the last stages of my most recent book; and learning how to be accessible without being overextended when I had my second child were all huge moments for me when I learned to balance what everyone else needed with what I needed, and I felt very good about that.

Potential Outcomes: What's the worst thing that could happen if you mixed and matched your standards now? What's the best thing that could happen?

The worst thing that could happen is that I feel uncomfortable and focus more on what I'm not doing than what I'm doing well. The best thing that could happen is that mixing and matching my standards makes it possible to give myself fully to those pursuits that matter most to me and that I can maintain high standards in these areas.

Transformers

Talk-Over #1: How can you talk to yourself in a new way about letting go that gives you a more flexible approach to achieving balance in your life?

I can say: "The more specific I am about how I'm willing to lower my standards, the easier it will be to lower them in the ways that bother me the least."

Talk-Over #2: How can you talk to yourself in a new way about holding on that gives you a more flexible approach to achieving balance in your life?

I can say: "By choosing to hold myself to high standards I'm increasing the likelihood that I'll be perceived as a high achiever on both the work and family fronts. The tradeoff is that I'm also increasing my risk of giving away too much power to others. I can still keep high standards while setting better boundaries about being accountable to others."

Conversation #56: Mixing And Matching Your Standards

Explorers

Letting Go:

Holding On:

Confidence-Builders

Life Lessons:

Potential Outcomes:

Transformers

Talk-Over #1:

Talk-Over #2:

Conversation #57: Saying "No" To Impossible Demands

Explorers

Just One More Thing: How do you react when your co-workers or family members ask you to do work that you think is excessive?

I usually either react by doing the work willingly, because it's the right thing to do; do it willingly if it's likely to be a one-time thing; or don't do it and feel guilty because I'm too busy.

Yesterday Deadlines: How do you handle it when your co-workers and family members ask you to do things with unrealistic deadlines?

I usually handle it by meeting the deadlines no matter what it takes or by discussing the situation with the deadline-setters.

Confidence-Builders

Life Lessons: What three times have you felt good about yourself as a result of setting limits about unreasonable amounts or time frames for work and family activities?

I felt good when I successfully negotiated an unrealistic deadline for a major project, because I believed strongly that the original one would compromise the quality of the work. When I set limits about how many house management-related responsibilities I was willing to take on, I felt good about making sure I didn't end up doing excessive amounts of these tasks. When I made sure that my contract terms for several projects included reasonable amounts of time to accomplish various parts of the process, I felt good about anticipating my future needs and taking the pressure off myself.

Potential Outcomes: What's the worst thing that could happen if you started consistently setting limits now? What's the best thing that could happen?

The worst thing that could happen is that I could upset or alienate others, and have to deal with strained relationships or lost opportunities. The best thing that could happen is that I could earn others' respect by sticking up for myself about how much work I do and when I do it.

Transformers

Talk-Over #1: How can you talk to yourself in a new way about just one more thing that gives you a more flexible approach to achieving balance in your life?

I can say: "I don't have to be a martyr to be a good worker and mom."

Talk-Over #2: How can you talk to yourself in a new way about yesterday deadlines that gives you a more flexible approach to achieving balance in your life?

I can say: "I have the power to decide on a case-by-case basis to meet certain deadlines, and I can also prevent many last minute hassles by working with my colleagues and family to plan ahead as much as possible."

Conversation #57: Saying "No" To Impossible Demands

Explorers

Just One More Thing:

Yesterday Deadlines:

Confidence-Builders

Life Lessons:

Potential Outcomes:

Transformers

Talk-Over #1:

Talk-Over #2:

Conversation #58: Streamlining Your Home Work

Explorers

Key Family Responsibilities: What must-do family tasks are you responsible for on a daily, weekly, or monthly basis? Is the balance of work fairly distributed among your family members? If not, in what particular areas do you want help to free up some of your time?

> I'm responsible for the bills, the laundry, making the kids meals, driving to and from school, and organizing special events. I share responsibilities for child care, buying clothes, maintaining family relationships, buying holiday presents, food shopping, dealing with the dry cleaning, and keeping the house tidy.

Time Busters: What aspects of your approach to your key family responsibilities could be more efficient?

> I could streamline when I pay the bills, when I make dinner, the laundry cycles, and when I get the kids ready to leave for school.

Confidence-Builders

Life Lessons: What three times have you felt good about yourself as a result of how you creatively managed your time at home?

> Having the whole family discuss making the most of our time and taking care of our responsibilities; ordering more necessities by phone and via the Internet; and establishing more clearly defined routines made me feel good about managing my time at home as efficiently as possible.

Potential Outcomes: What's the worst thing that could happen if you tried to manage your time better by redistributing some of your family work and by streamlining your approach to it? What's the best thing that could happen?

> The worst thing that could happen is that I have to adjust to things not always being done my way and expect that others will have to adjust to new responsibilities and ways of doing things too.

Transformers

Talk-Over #1: How can you talk to yourself in a new way about your key family responsibilities that gives you a more flexible approach to balancing your career?

> I can say: "My husband and I are a team and can make sure that family tasks are divided equally between us in the context of our work and family responsibilities as a whole."

Talk-Over #2: How can you talk to yourself in a new way about time busters that gives you a more flexible approach to balancing your career?

> I can say: "There are always ways that I can improve how efficiently I complete household tasks. By trying new approaches as well as getting ideas from friends, magazine articles, and time management books, I can streamline my home work."

Conversation #58: Streamlining Your Home Work

Explorers

Key Family Responsibilities:

Time Busters:

Confidence-Builders

Life Lessons:

Potential Outcomes:

Transformers

Talk-Over #1:

Talk-Over #2:

Conversation #59: Cloning Yourself

Explorers

Personalizing Your Systems: What things that you do enable you to virtually be in two places at once?

> I put love notes in the kids' lunches; post information about important family activities and appointments on the refrigerator; document my work projects in detail; and keep my work and personal files up to date and in order.

Balancing Act Partners: Who do you depend on in your work and personal lives as your allies?

> I depend on an inner circle of close family members, friends, colleagues, mentors, and school staff, among others, as my allies.

Confidence-Builders

Life Lessons: What three times have you felt good about yourself as a result of how you cloned yourself through systems or partners?

> When I documented a complex work project in detail; accepted one of my best friends' generous offer to watch my oldest child in a crisis; and put love notes in my daughter's lunch during a transition time for her I felt good about how I cloned myself.

Potential Outcomes: What's the worst thing that could happen if you cloned yourself more both through systems and partners? What's the best thing that could happen?

> The worst thing that could happen is that I feel less needed directly. The best thing that could happen is that I'm able to be there more for my family and colleagues without having to rush around or try to be in two places at once as much.

Transformers

Talk-Over #1: How can you talk to yourself in a new way about personalizing your systems that gives you a more flexible approach to balancing your career?

> I can say: "It would improve the quality of my work and family relationships if I put into place more ways to communicate with the important people in my life even when I'm not physically there."

Talk-Over #2: How can you talk to yourself in a new way about balancing act partners that gives you a more flexible approach to balancing your career?

> I can say: "I need to acknowledge my partners on a regular basis with cards or notes; token gifts; and making sure I'm giving them what they need in return. I can also strengthen the quality of my partnerships by making sure that the people whom I choose as partners are compatible with me in terms of our values, approach, and personality style as much as possible."

Conversation #59: Cloning Yourself

Explorers

Personalizing Your Systems:

Balancing Act Partners:

Confidence-Builders

Life Lessons:

Potential Outcomes:

Transformers

Talk-Over #1:

Talk-Over #2:

Conversation #60: Springing The Comparison Trap

Explorers

The Set-Up: When do you most often compare yourself to other working moms?

> When I talk with other working moms about our lives or read about other working moms in magazine articles, I most often compare myself to them.

The Fall: About what do you usually compare yourself to other working moms?

> I usually compare myself to other working moms about my physical appearance, my state of mind, or my level of work-family balance satisfaction.

Confidence-Builders

Life Lessons: What three times have you felt good about yourself as a result of how you either stopped yourself from or didn't feel bad about yourself by comparing yourself to other working moms?

> After I had my first child, I stopped myself from comparing myself with other working moms' state of mind, since it became obvious that every situation is different. During a crossroads when I was redirecting my private practice, I stopped myself from comparing myself to other working moms about my level of work-family balance satisfaction. After the birth of my second child, I stopped myself from comparing my appearance with other working moms for a while.

Potential Outcomes: What's the worst thing that could happen if you minimized your self-destructive comparing now? What's the best thing that could happen?

> The worst thing that could happen is that I have to face either making constructive changes in my life or accepting myself and my life as is. The best thing that could happen is that I feel inspired to improve myself, bond with other working moms, and learn to love myself more regardless of what stage of growth I'm in.

Transformers

Talk-Over #1: How can you talk to yourself in a new way about the set-up that gives you a more flexible approach to balancing your career?

> I can say: "By seeking to learn about other working moms' struggles as well as their accomplishments, I can keep my own challenges and self-doubts in perspective."

Talk-Over #2: How can you talk to yourself in a new way about the fall that gives you a more flexible approach to balancing your career?

> I can say: "Instead of comparing myself to some working moms, I can look at them as sources of inspiration and ideas for how to improve the quality of my own life and self-image."

Conversation #60: Springing The Comparison Trap

Explorers

The Set-Up:

The Fall:

Confidence-Builders

Life Lessons:

Potential Outcomes:

Transformers

Talk-Over #1:

Talk-Over #2:

IDENTITY: Integrating Your Selves

7

The Conversations
- Re-titling yourself
- Making over your transitions
- Projecting self-confidence
- Managing perceptions about your double life
- Planning for the blues
- Making processing time
- Blurring the boundaries
- Counting higher than two
- Separating and equalizing your selves
- Activating working mom resources
- Finding the complimentary angles
- Playing non-competitive games

Traditional portrayals of working moms in the mass media often have branded us as either "fast-trackers" or "mommy-trackers"—misfits who can't fully fit into either their work or home communities, and who chronically complain about being overwhelmed by our dual lives. But these stereotypes are being replaced by the informal "campaigns" of contemporary working moms to find a better fit between work and home life. And even the media is beginning to present more integrated portrayals that recognize working moms' efforts.

Coordinating Your Roles

Television, movies, books, and even advertisements have shown us working moms who have been more committed to their career (fast trackers), and moms who have been more committed to their families (mommy trackers). But, what the media has not been so great about demonstrating is that working moms can be equally devoted to both career and family. Instead of separating your worker and mom identities, treating them as if they are competing for your time and energy, you can strive to integrate them. One way to do this is by focusing on what is most meaningful to you in each of these roles and discovering how each one adds value to the other. Another way is to make the transitions between your work and family lives as smooth as possible—intellectually, physically, and spiritually.

But it's sometimes hard to manage this change in attitude and lifestyle. Working moms often feel misunderstood by their non-mom colleagues, who don't share many of the special needs, responsibilities and issues that working moms face. And they feel equally misunderstood by stay-at-home moms who don't always understand the professional side of the working mom's life.

Creating New Perceptions

Managing both a career and family doesn't have to make you feel alienated and alone. You can refocus others' faulty—or even negative—perceptions by reacting constructively, rather than defensively, to them. You can find common ground with colleagues in your career and with other moms by taking an active interest in their lives as well as sharing your own—through collaborating at work or on community projects; by seeking advice; by sincerely complimenting others on their efforts; and by swapping appropriate stories at the right times. The point is to open up to others as an individual—revealing yourself as someone who is more than just the "worker" and "mom" personas that help define you.

Often, working moms have been stereotyped as being fixated solely on their concerns or difficulties about their dual roles, and they have been characterized as insecure, depressed, and stressed-out to the max. You can counter this negative image by projecting self-confidence; planning for both the predictable and unpredictable blues; making processing time, finding or creating resources; reminding yourself about how both you and those whose lives you touch benefit from your being a working mom; and amplifying the fun parts of both of your roles. To do this, you'll need to look carefully at the way you integrate your professional and personal identities.

In these conversations, you'll discover new ways to feel less fragmented by integrating your worker and mom identities. And, my thoughts and feelings about dealing with identity issues are just a little to your left. So if you're having trouble getting started on a question, you're welcome to see how I approached it.

Conversation #61: Re-titling Yourself

Explorers

Reviewing Your Job Descriptions: What subtitles describe your responsibilities as a worker? As a mom?

> My career subtitles include: idea-generator, researcher, wordsmith, editor, curriculum developer, public speaker, facilitator, evaluator, listener, advisor, coach, and resource-provider. Some of my subtitles as a mom include: self-esteem booster, coach, nurturer, safety officer, mediator, storyteller, advisor, medic, accountant, personal shopper, decorator, party planner, chauffeur, and chef.

Playing the Name Game: Now that you've listed your work and mom subtitles, how do your priorities as both a professional and as a mom overlap? What's a new, integrated title for you instead of "working mom" that reflects how you handle both sets of priorities?

> When my priorities overlap completely, then I'd create one title, like "Creativity Diva" or "Conflict Resolution Guru." When I have two different priorities, then I'd create a combined title like "Strategic Planning Expert" and "Storytelling Whiz." If I have one overlapping priority and a different one, then I'd create a different combined title, like "Community-Building Specialist" and "Director of Wellness."

Confidence-Builders

Life Lessons: What three times have you felt good about yourself as a result of realizing all that you really do in your roles as a working mom or prioritizing what's really special to you among these roles?

> I felt good about realizing what I really do as a working mom and prioritizing what's most important to me among my roles after the birth of each of my children as well as right before deciding to have a second child.

Potential Outcomes: What's the worst thing that could happen if you retitled yourself based on your priorities now? What's the best thing that could happen?

> The worst thing would be to feel vulnerable by putting my true self out there and risking rejection. The best thing would be to clearly define my current self based on what I value the most and make wise decisions based on this redefinition.

Transformers

Talk-Over #1: How can you talk to yourself in a new way about reviewing your job descriptions that gives you a more flexible approach to integrating your two selves?

> I can say: "I am proud of the many different roles that I play, and I refuse to expend energy questioning myself about why I can't do more."

Talk-Over #2: How can you talk to yourself in a new way about playing the name game that gives you a more flexible approach to integrating your two selves?

> I can say: "Giving myself a name other than "working mom" is powerful, because it helps me to perceive myself as a unique, strong, and integrated person."

Conversation #61: Re-titling Yourself

Explorers

Reviewing Your Job Descriptions:

Playing the Name Game:

Confidence-Builders

Life Lessons:

Potential Outcomes:

Transformers

Talk-Over #1:

Talk-Over #2:

Conversation #62: Making Over Your Transitions

Explorers

Strengthening Exercises: How do you currently make transitions between your work and family mindsets as smooth as possible?

> I try to make mental transitions by announcing to myself that it's time to move from one world to the other. I usually make physical transitions between my worlds by changing clothes, or putting on or taking off a symbolic item like a hat or watch. And I regularly make spiritual transitions by spending time at least every morning and evening to practice my personal version of spiritual connection.

Space Lifts: How do you currently make space transitions as smooth as possible between work and family?

> I transition into my work space by putting out special items and doing little rituals to enter my work zone, and transition out of it by putting away my work, tidying my desk and closing my computer. I transition into my living space by diving into a family activity like baking with my children, arranging fresh flowers, putting on my favorite music, or having a picnic.

Confidence-Builders

Life Lessons: What three times have you felt good about yourself as a result of simplifying or increasing the versatility of your transitions?

> When I simplified my work and personal computer systems to facilitate quicker entries and exits; developed portable, mini work packets; and revamped my wardrobe to fit both worlds I felt good about improving my transitions between work and family.

Potential Outcomes: What's the worst thing that could happen if you made over your transitions now? What's the best thing that could happen?

> The worst thing that could happen is that I discover that to truly improve my transitions, I have to slow down and pace myself better, which is hard for me to do. The best thing that could happen is that I feel like I'm living a more integrated, comfortable life.

Transformers

Talk-Over #1: How can you talk to yourself in a new way about personal toning and strengthening exercises that gives you a more flexible approach to integrating your two selves?

> I can say: "I need to establish firm transitions between work and home so that I can fully dedicate myself to each, when the time is right. These transitions need to cover all the bases: mental, physical, and spiritual."

Talk-Over #2: How can you talk to yourself in a new way about space lifts that gives you a more flexible approach to integrating your two selves?

> I can say: "If I allow for a little overlap of family space into work space—and vice versa—my transitions can become much smoother, and it will make it easier for me when I have to be able to do both at the same time."

Conversation #62: Making Over Your Transitions

Explorers

Strengthening Exercises:

Space Lifts:

Confidence-Builders

Life Lessons:

Potential Outcomes:

Transformers

Talk-Over #1:

Talk-Over #2:

Conversation #63: Projecting Self-Confidence

Explorers

Defining the Big "It": How do you define "self-confidence" in terms of how you would look, sound, and feel as a self-confident person?

As a self-confident person, I'd appear calm under pressure; sound passionate about my convictions; and feel that anything is possible because I'm powerful.

Role Models: Which self-confident person or people who you know or admire from afar would you like to emulate and why?

I admire Barbara Sher, because I appreciate and respect her courage to make her vision become a reality and because she writes with conviction and passion grounded in real-life experience as a way to empower others. But I also would like to emulate Michelle Tullier, because I admire her for being a savvy, calculated risk-taker and entrepreneur whose genuine words and strategic actions earn her widespread respect.

Confidence-Builders

Life Lessons: What three times have you felt good about yourself as a result of projecting self-confidence?

When I conduct workshops, get interviewed by the media, and negotiate book contracts, I've felt good about my ability to project self-confidence—even when I'm nervous beforehand about how I'm going to come across to others.

Potential Outcomes: What's the worst thing that could happen if you developed more self-confidence and more ways to project it now? What's the best thing that could happen?

The worst thing that could happen is that I come on too strong and appear to be cocky, or make others feel overwhelmed or threatened by me. The best thing that could happen is that I can inspire others to take confident action in their lives, as well as feel more self-confident to pursue my goals.

Transformers

Talk-Over #1: How can you talk to yourself in a new way about projecting the big "it" that gives you a more flexible approach to integrating your two selves?

I can say: "My definition of self-confidence should encompass how I feel about myself, and I should express these feelings through how I look and sound. I can develop more self-confidence by working on my inner self and letting it affect my outer self."

Talk-Over #2: How can you talk to yourself in a new way about role models that gives you a more flexible approach to integrating your two selves?

I can say: "By choosing confident role models who have similar personality styles to mine I can better imitate how they project self-confidence through their personal mannerisms."

Conversation #63: Projecting Self-Confidence

Explorers

Defining the Big "It":

Role Models:

Confidence-Builders

Life Lessons:

Potential Outcomes:

Transformers

Talk-Over #1:

Talk-Over #2:

Conversation #64: Managing Perceptions About Your Double Life

Explorers

Same Stuff, Different Day: What negative perceptions about being a working mom do you observe, hear remarks about, or feel vibes about at work?

> Working from home, I haven't had to deal with negative perceptions from work-world people directly in my work environment. But I have heard lots of complaints from other people about employers giving preferential treatment to workers without family commitments and about how unfair it is that working moms get more flack about time off.

The Continental Divide: What negative perceptions about being a working mom do you observe, especially among stay-at-home moms?

> Although I've been lucky with a very supportive community, I have heard of stay-at-home moms who have banded together to make sure working moms don't get voted into PTA officer positions; overheard conversations about how working moms are selfish and their kids are suffering because of their work lives; and sensed that they're not fully welcome to become close friends with the clique of stay-at-home moms because they're not living through the same bonding experiences.

Confidence-Builders

Life Lessons: What three times have you felt good about yourself as a result of managing others' misconceptions about your abilities as a working mom?

> Three times when I've had to manage others' misconceptions about my abilities as a working mom were when I proved that I was still running a legitimate business even if it did become home-based; when I convinced friends that protecting my work time at home wasn't being anti-social; and when I clearly let everybody know that my commitment to my family was my top priority.

Potential Outcomes: What's the worst thing that could happen if you focused on managing others' misconceptions in more constructive ways now? What's the best thing that could happen?

> The worst thing would be to spend excessive time and effort trying to explain myself. The best thing is that I might avoid becoming defensive, and help build stronger communities among all types of moms.

Transformers

Talk-Over #1: How can you talk to yourself in a new way about same stuff different day that gives you a more flexible approach to integrating your two selves?

> I can say: "When I feel affected by negative perceptions about my status as a working mom, I can react constructively by trying to advocate work-family friendly attitudes."

Talk-Over #2: How can you talk to yourself in a new way about the continental divide that gives you a more flexible approach to integrating your two selves?

> I can say: "I'll collaborate more on community projects, focus on common ground issues, and make every effort to get to know others and have them get to know me."

Conversation #64: Managing Perceptions About Your Double Life

Explorers

Same Stuff, Different Day:

The Continental Divide:

Confidence-Builders

Life Lessons:

Potential Outcomes:

Transformers

Talk-Over #1:

Talk-Over #2:

Conversation #65: Planning For The Blues

Explorers

Blue Notes: What are some of the predictable blues in your work and personal lives? How do you plan for and cope with these blues?

> In my work life, post-crunch times are the hardest because they leave me feeling drained. So I try to avoid intense deadlines and when I can't, weave in some pampering to renew myself. In my personal life, holiday planning times are often challenging for me. So I try to plan for these blues by making it a family effort and keeping the tone of the holidays low-key.

Out-of-the-Blue Blues: What are some unpredictable types of blues in your work and personal lives? How do you usually cope with these kinds of blues?

> Sudden deadlines, unforeseen burnout, and sick family members are among the unpredictable types of blues in my work and personal lives. I usually cope with these kinds of blues by reminding myself that the best things I can do are to be as proactive as possible about preventing them from happening; that I can choose how to react to them; and that the crises will pass as they have before.

Confidence-Builders

Life Lessons: What three times have you felt good about yourself as a result of how you've planned for or coped with both predictable and unpredictable blues?

> When I've planned for an especially difficult work deadline; dealt with a stressful holiday gathering; and coped with an unforeseen family illness, I've felt good about myself for how I've handled both predictable and unpredictable blues.

Potential Outcomes: What's the worst thing that could happen if you planned better for handling predictable and unpredictable blues now? What's the best thing that could happen?

> The worst thing that could happen is that I could defeat myself by setting unrealistic expectations in the face of unexpected problems. The best thing that could happen is that I have more resources in place to minimize my levels of stress as a working mom.

Transformers

Talk-Over #1: How can you talk to yourself in a new way about blue notes that gives you a more flexible approach to integrating your two selves?

> I can say: "I can develop more creative resources to prevent and minimize predictable blues times."

Talk-Over #2: How can you talk to yourself in a new way about out-of-the-blue blues that gives you a more flexible approach to integrating your two selves?

> I can say: "By simplifying my life to the core basics and communicating with my family about the time frame and our collective needs during this challenge, I can minimize the intensity of out-of-the-blue blues, and get through it conserving as much energy as possible."

Conversation #65: Planning For The Blues

Explorers

Blue Notes:

Out-of-the-Blue Blues:

Confidence-Builders

Life Lessons:

Potential Outcomes:

Transformers

Talk-Over #1:

Talk-Over #2:

Conversation #66: Making Processing Time

Explorers

Finding the Time: When do you make time to you check in with yourself and sort through your issues as a working mom?

> I usually check in with myself about my working mom issues during my early morning writing time, a long shower, or while chatting with friends.

Figuring Out What's Up: How do you prepare to go through the process? How do you become aware of your issues?

> Listening to relaxing music, taking a nature walk, and asking myself what's up are usually the ways that I prepare to process my feelings about being a working mom.

Confidence-Builders

Life Lessons: What three times have you felt good about yourself as a result of making time to process your issues as a working mom?

> After my first child was born, I had lots of chats with friends; during a major crossroads between my two children's births, I made consistent morning time; and after the birth of my second child, I made time for showers dedicated to letting my feelings surface and releasing them.

Potential Outcomes: What's the worst thing that could happen if you made processing time as much of a habit as brushing your teeth now? What's the best thing that could happen?

The worst thing that could happen is that I may feel frustrated if I can't immediately resolve my problems. The best thing that could happen is that I don't let negative feelings eat away at me too long, let small problems snowball into big ones, or face patterns of recurring issues.

Transformers

Talk-Over #1: How can you talk to yourself in a new way about finding the time that gives you a more flexible approach to integrating your two selves?

> I can say: "It's valuable to set aside even five minutes regularly to deal with my thoughts and feelings about being a working mom so they don't build up and become overwhelming. If I really want to, I can make the time for decompressing."

Talk-Over #2: How can you talk to yourself in a new way about figuring out what's up that gives you a more flexible approach to integrating your two selves?

> I can say: "I can best discover my issues and goals about being a working mom by processing them in the way that's most comfortable for me."

Conversation #66: Making Processing Time

Explorers

Finding the Time:

Figuring Out What's Up:

Confidence-Builders

Life Lessons:

Potential Outcomes:

Transformers

Talk-Over #1:

Talk-Over #2:

Conversation #67: Blurring The Boundaries

Explorers

Mom-at-Work: What types of anecdotes do you usually share with your colleagues and family members about your other lives?

> During work hours, I sometimes share stories about my children's achievements and offbeat house "disasters." In my personal life, I sometimes share my personal success stories and funny bloopers.

Around the Edges: When do you usually swap stories with colleagues and family members?

> During work hours I sometimes swap stories, for example, at the end of phone conversations when it's appropriate and I have the time. At home, I usually share stories during catch-up times—often at dinner or over the weekend.

Confidence-Builders

Life Lessons: What three times have you felt good about yourself as a result of sharing challenging, funny, or meaningful events from your work life with your family members and from your family life with your co-workers?

> When I spent an afternoon talking with other working moms over brunch about the challenges of our lives; hosted a success-sharing celebration with my family; and spent an hour with my husband laughing at the lighter side of my work life craziness, I felt good about blurring the boundaries between my work and family lives.

Potential Outcomes: What's the worst thing that could happen if you more fully integrated your work and home lives through selective storytelling now? What's the best thing that could happen?

> The worst thing that could happen is that I blur the boundaries too much. The best thing that could happen is that I become more genuine, understood, and connected at work and at home.

Transformers

Talk-Over #1: How can you talk to yourself in a new way about mom-at-work that gives you a more flexible approach to integrating your two selves?

> I can say: "By sharing stories about the other part of my life, I can integrate both my worker and mom selves most effectively. Also, I can guard my privacy by making sure my stories at work aren't too personal and respect my family by making sure my stories at home aren't too negative or full of complaining."

Talk-Over #2: How can you talk to yourself in a new way about around the edges that gives you a more flexible approach to integrating your two selves?

> I can say: "When I share stories is equally important to what I share, since sharing stories at work from my home life could be give me a reputation as a time-buster and sharing stories at home from my work life randomly could be perceived as bringing work home too much."

Conversation #67: Blurring The Boundaries

Explorers

Mom-at-Work:

Around the Edges:

Confidence-Builders

Life Lessons:

Potential Outcomes:

Transformers

Talk-Over #1:

Talk-Over #2:

Conversation #68: Counting Higher Than Two

Explorers

Beyond "Working Mom": What other aspects of your identity as a person besides "worker" and "mom" help define you?

My gender, ethnicity, marital status, and spiritual beliefs help define me.

Putting the Puzzle Together: How do the pieces of your identity as a working mom fit into your identity as whole person?

At this point in my life, I see my working mom pieces as prominent and defining—framing, multi-colored, irregularly-shaped, big pieces of my identity puzzle.

Confidence-Builders

Life Lessons: What three times have you felt good about yourself as a result of recognizing and meeting your needs as a whole person?

When I took time to explore my ethnic identity and what it meant to me; to find creative ways to have more "date" time with my husband given our full career and home lives; and to ensure that I practiced my spirituality every day I felt good about respecting my needs as a whole person.

Potential Outcomes: What's the worst thing that could happen if you perceived the multiple parts of your identity as interrelated now? What's the best thing that could happen?

The worst thing that could happen is that I discover that I need to do some intensive inner work to figure out what means most to me and how to meet those needs. The best thing that could happen is that I step back and see the big picture of myself as a whole person and feel more complete.

Transformers

Talk-Over #1: How can you talk to yourself in a new way about beyond "working mom" that gives you a more flexible approach to integrating your two selves?

I can say: "The many parts of my identity have different origins—some by birth, some by choice, and some by circumstance—but they are all important and make me who I am to myself and how I represent myself to others."

Talk-Over #2: How can you talk to yourself in a new way about putting the puzzle together that gives you a more flexible approach to integrating your two selves?

I can say: "At different times in my life, some pieces of my identity are more important than other pieces to me and to others. But at all times they fit together to form an integrated picture of me."

Conversation #68: Counting Higher Than Two

Explorers

Beyond "Working Mom":

Putting the Puzzle Together:

Confidence-Builders

Life Lessons:

Potential Outcomes:

Transformers

Talk-Over #1:

Talk-Over #2:

Conversation #69: Separating And Equalizing Your Selves

Explorers

Integrating versus Fusing: Day to day, do you strive to fuse (working-mom) or to integrate (working mom) your worker and mom selves? What are the challenges of your approach?

> I sometimes try to merge my worker and mom identities into a single entity, since the demands of my worlds are often so mixed together. But—on a practical as well as emotional level—it's impossible to fully blend together my two roles, since they're not identical and need their own special kinds of attention and nurturing to fully blossom.

Being Fully Present: How do you let yourself fully experience each of your roles as worker and as mom?

> I immerse myself in each of my roles by, for example, adopting tunnel vision so that I'm not distracted by piles of laundry when I'm working, or e-mails when I'm with my family; and putting physical distance between my home stuff and me when I'm working, and between my work stuff and me when I'm with my family.

Confidence-Builders

Life Lessons: What three times have you felt good about yourself as a result of separating and equalizing your roles as a working mom?

> When I managed to be fully present with my family on our last vacation; be fully present during writing sessions while finishing my last book; and let my worker and mom selves co-habitate peacefully after my second child was born, I felt good about equalizing and separating my roles as a working mom.

Potential Outcomes: What's the worst thing that could happen if you separated and equalized your roles as a working mom all of the time now? What's the best thing that could happen?

> The worst thing that could happen is that I find it hard to separate my roles and concentrate fully on whichever world I'm in at the time. The best thing that could happen is that when I need to make a change in my career and life balance, it won't have to be big deal.

Transformers

Talk-Over #1: How can you talk to yourself in a new way about integrating versus fusing that gives you a more flexible approach to integrating your two selves?

> I can say: "By striving to integrate, rather than to fuse, my roles as a worker and as a mom, they can co-exist harmoniously rather than suffocate each other."

Talk-Over #2: How can you talk to yourself in a new way about being fully present that gives you a more flexible approach to integrating your two selves?

> I can say: "By honoring the present moment, I generate a positive, centered energy that nurtures the bond between my worker and mom selves. When I allow myself to get distracted unnecessarily by somewhere else or someone else I'm not at the time, I generate a negative, fragmented energy that weakens this bond."

Conversation #69: Separating And Equalizing Your Selves

Explorers

Integrating versus Fusing:

Being Fully Present:

Confidence-Builders

Life Lessons:

Potential Outcomes:

Transformers

Talk-Over #1:

Talk-Over #2:

Conversation #70: Activating Working Mom Resources

Explorers

Designated Drivers: What working mom resources are you aware of or use to help you guide your career and grow your family?

> I'm aware of or use a variety of working mom resources, including books, magazines, newsletters, web sites, support groups, and mentoring networks.

Finding Your Way Home: What challenges do you face for which there are limited or no targeted resources that you're aware of?

> The umbrella challenge that I face—and have faced at every crossroads since becoming a working mom—concerns how to adapt my career to my lifestyle.

Confidence-Builders

Life Lessons: What three times have you felt good about yourself as a result of using working mom resources to improve the quality of your life?

> When I've participated in support networks with other working moms, read magazine articles about hot working mom issues, and used websites as resources for addressing my issues as a working mom, I've felt good about actively helping myself.

Potential Outcomes: What's the worst thing that could happen if you sought or created more resources for yourself now? What's the best thing that could happen?

> The worst thing that could happen is that I discover that I'm overwhelmed by the process or have accidentally duplicated existing resources. The best thing that could happen is that I feel more self-reliant in terms of my ability to find solutions to my problems and more connected to other working moms.

Transformers

Talk-Over #1: How can you talk to yourself in a new way about designated drivers that gives you a more flexible approach to integrating your two selves?

> I can say: "I can find the time and patience to sort through the various resources that might be helpful to me as a working mom by, for example, book-marking and organizing web sites in a favorites file; setting aside a designated time slot each day or week to skim potential resources to see if they're valuable; and prioritizing which specific resources are most important."

Talk-Over #2: How can you talk to yourself in a new way about finding your way home that gives you a more flexible approach to integrating your two selves?

> I can say: "Chances are that just because I don't know of a resource to help me with a specific working mom issue, it still may exist."

Conversation #70: Activating Working Mom Resources

Explorers

Designated Drivers:

Finding Your Way Home:

Confidence-Builders

Life Lessons:

Potential Outcomes:

Transformers

Talk-Over #1:

Talk-Over #2:

Conversation #71: Finding The Complementary Angles

Explorers

Respecting Your Selves: How do you benefit in terms of your personal growth from being a working mom?

> I benefit from being a working mom intellectually by feeling stimulated in two different ways; physically by needing to maintain good health and stamina in order to keep up with both of my roles; emotionally by being challenged to grow, and spiritually by fulfilling my need for meaningful work in which I can both express myself and serve others in two venues.

Valuing Your Contributions: How do your colleagues and family members benefit from your being a working mom?

> My colleagues and family members benefit from my being a working mom because I'm a happier person this way and, in turn, have more to offer both sets of people on many levels.

Confidence-Builders

Life Lessons: What three times have you felt good about yourself as a result of how you contributed to your and others' development by being a working mom?

> When I challenged myself to become more flexible both at work and at home as a new working mom; shared how it's possible to pursue my passions through my work with my family; and applied my real-life experience as a working mom to my work, I felt good about how I contributed to my as well as others' development as a working mom.

Potential Outcomes: What's the worst thing that could happen if you valued your identity as a working mom for how it has a positive impact on both yourself and others now? What's the best thing that could happen?

> The worst thing that could happen is that I just accept that I need to keep evaluating whether or not the pluses for me and others outweigh the minuses. The best thing that could happen is that I confirm that—for now, anyway—being a working mom is an asset to me and others around me.

Transformers

Talk-Over #1: How can you talk to yourself in a new way about respecting your selves that gives you a more flexible approach to integrating your two selves?

> I can say: "The challenges of integrating my worker and mom selves is worth it, because through experiencing both roles and facing the challenges, I grow on so many levels."

Talk-Over #2: How can you talk to yourself in a new way about valuing your contributions that gives you a more flexible approach to integrating your two selves?

> I can say: "As a working mom, I bring a unique set of resources to both my work and family worlds."

Conversation #71: Finding The Complementary Angles

Explorers

Respecting Your Selves:

Valuing Your Contributions:

Confidence-Builders

Life Lessons:

Potential Outcomes:

Transformers

Talk-Over #1:

Talk-Over #2:

Conversation #72: Playing Non-Competitive Games

Explorers

Belly Laughs: What are the most fun, playful activities in your work and family lives?

> The most fun, playful activities in my work life include getting to know new people, writing, and learning about new, exciting adventures. In my family life they include storytelling, role-playing, art, cloud-watching, and water and sand play, and climbing.

Free-for-Alls: How could you transfer play activities between your work and family lives to maximize the kinds and amount you have in both overall?

> Overall, I could remember to adopt a more playful attitude in both of my lives, especially since I tend to be a fun, but intense, person. Specifically, I could transfer my play activities between my work and family lives by making even more of an effort to reach out to and get to know other people in our neighborhood. I could transfer my play activities between my family and work lives by incorporating some of my family's favorite play activities into my creative brainstorming process for my writing, counseling, and teaching activities.

Confidence-Builders

Life Lessons: What three times have you felt good about yourself as a result of enjoying the lighter side of your work and family lives?

> When I spent the afternoon jumping waves in the ocean and playing in the sand with my family; cooking an improvised feast with my family; and socializing—no work talk allowed—with my close colleagues, I felt good about lightening up in my family and work lives.

Potential Outcomes: What's the worst thing that could happen if you focused more on having fun rather than on being superworker and supermom now? What's the best thing that could happen?

> The worst that could happen is that I overindulge in play. The best thing that could happen is that I become less intense and driven, enjoy life more, and both my work and family lives benefit from this more playful approach.

Transformers

Talk-Over #1: How can you talk to yourself in a new way about belly laughs that gives you a more flexible approach to integrating your two selves?

> I can say: "It's often the little things that help me to have fun and make a difference in my day."

Talk-Over #2: How can you talk to yourself in a new way about free-for-alls that gives you a more flexible approach to integrating your two selves?

> I can say: "When I commit myself to having fun every day in both my work and personal lives, then play and pleasure become part of my common ground between my worker and mom selves."

Conversation #72: Playing Non-Competitive Games

Explorers

Belly Laughs:

Free-for-Alls:

Confidence-Builders

Life Lessons:

Potential Outcomes:

Transformers

Talk-Over #1:

Talk-Over #2:

SUPPORT: Making It After All

8

The Conversations
- Forming alliances on both sides
- Grouping and backing up your systems
- Surrounding yourself with positive people
- Giving up martyrdom and guessing games
- Gathering wisdom hand-me-downs
- Using your life history as a life raft
- Managing your assets
- Befriending your creative muse
- Approaching your challenges as invitations
- Fostering your communities
- Grounding yourself in what's meaningful
- Trusting the process

For a long time, support for working moms was hard to come by, for several reasons. First of all, society in general has long refused to recognize that formal, accessible resources for working moms are a priority. It's been quick to assume that we can, and should, work these things out for ourselves. Second, many employers have been slow to recognize just how advantageous it would be—to them—if they offered real support. And third, many working moms have been reluctant to ask for help because we believed that we didn't deserve it, or were simply too proud to confess that we needed it.

But these attitudes are changing. Many modern organizations have learned that providing support for working moms is a win-win deal. And even less enlightened organizations have begun to face the powerful, articulate demands of their working-mom employees. In all areas of the work world, contemporary working moms have been coming up with approaches that acknowledge our complex, ever-changing needs.

Assessing What's Out There

Working moms employed in traditional organizations have begun to demand such support systems as on-site or back-up childcare centers; career-development counseling and mentoring programs; commuting subsidies or transportation services; and wellness programs. We see that many progressive organizations already have developed some or all of these programs, because those organizations have come to recognize the value of reducing working moms' stress levels.

They're reaping their reward for such programs through lower absenteeism and increased worker productivity—which have had a positive impact on the organizations' bottom lines. As the benefits of these policies become increasingly obvious, more organizations are following suit.

But even if you work for an organization that doesn't yet offer such programs, you do have options. You can join forces with professional colleagues and friends or family. You can develop back-up systems to cover your support needs, and you can surround yourself exclusively with people who have a positive attitude toward working moms.

Finding Your Own Solutions

Some working moms feel uncomfortable seeking help because they believe they should be able to handle all of these responsibilities solo. Others don't want to be a burden, so they struggle alone and hope that someone will offer to help. But you don't have to suffer in silence. It's okay to ask for help when you know you need it. In fact, it's particularly useful to seek advice from a variety of other working mothers. That way you're more likely to learn new ways to manage your support issues. And if you nurture your work and home communities, you'll create a solid foundation of mutual support in both places.

Finally, working moms often underestimate their own resources. By taking a few basic steps, however, you can increase your sense of self-reliance on all fronts: emotionally, financially, creatively, and spiritually. You can review your life history for personal "heroine tales"—times in the past when you've successfully overcome challenges. These will inspire you to try new ways to resolve current problems. If you're worried that you can't make a go of it financially, you can learn how to maximize your income. And you can explore creative approaches to everyday work and family activities.

One key to achieving all this is to perceive your challenges as chances to grow. Also, by grounding yourself in what's meaningful to you and trusting the process of your evolving needs and opportunities, you'll find that help will come to you. In this chapter you'll explore new approaches to getting the support you need by developing strong support networks and becoming more self-reliant. And, once again, I'll be exploring all these possibilities too, in case you need some help along the way.

Conversation #73: Forming Alliances On Both Sides

Explorers

Your Inner Circle: Who are your key allies in your personal life? How about in your professional life?

My key allies when I'm dealing with personal issues come from my family, but my close friends—both from college and later—are also great sources of support. Our pediatrician and the staff at the pre-school have all contributed greatly. I'd also have to include my professional mentors and several close colleagues.

Keeping the Peace: How do you maintain good relationships with your allies? How do you deal with any dissatisfaction or tension you experience?

I try to make sure that the balance between giving and taking is okay, and that I'm supporting my allies on their terms when they need it. Whenever tension creeps into these relationships, I try to determine whether what's wrong is really a big deal or not. I'll let go of the little things, but if it's important then I might sit down with my allies to discuss the problem objectively for both sides.

Confidence-Builders

Life Lessons: What three times have you felt good about yourself as a result of forming and maintaining solid alliances in your personal and professional lives?

Developing solid alliances with a couple of writing colleagues helped me stay focused and excited about my work. Discovering that my kids feel really comfortable with a couple of my close friends proved that my friendships were good for the whole family. The same is true about my daughter's pre-school staff—I really feel like they take a personal interest in her happiness and well-being.

Potential Outcomes: What's the worst thing that could happen if you more carefully selected and developed relationships with allies now? What's the best thing that could happen?

The worst thing that could happen is that some alliances may not work out and I may choose to end them. But that's nothing I can't overcome. The best thing that could happen is that I end up with a stable, long-term network of support.

Transformers

Talk-Over #1: How can you talk to yourself in a new way about your inner circle that gives you a more flexible approach to getting the support you need?

I can say: "It's okay to choose whom I depend on for support in my personal and professional lives, and I'm the best judge of the criteria I use in selecting them."

Talk-Over #2: How can you talk to yourself in a new way about keeping the peace that gives you a more flexible approach to getting the support you need?

I can say: "My relationships with my allies are partnerships, and that part of developing and maintaining healthy, long-term alliances requires showing my appreciation for my allies."

Conversation #73: Forming Alliances On Both Sides

Explorers

Your Inner Circle:

Keeping the Peace:

Confidence-Builders

Life Lessons:

Potential Outcomes:

Transformers

Talk-Over #1:

Talk-Over #2:

Conversation #74: Grouping And Backing Up Your Systems

Explorers

What Goes Together: For what types of issues do you regularly need support, and who do you normally rely on to handle them?

Getting my kids to and from school is the biggest issue that I need support in handling. Usually I rely on myself and my husband to take care of this. Getting the shopping done so that we've got the food, clothes, and work supplies we need when we need them is also important, and it's usually me or my husband who takes care of this. Finally there's the "emergency system"—asking our parents to pitch in.

Contingency Plans: What are your back-up arrangements for each primary system in case the regular one fails?

I've got a couple of friends who live nearby that I can call on for back-up transportation or extra help in a crisis. When my normal arrangements for running errands break down I turn to providers that will deliver the items I need.

Confidence-Builders

Life Lessons: What three times have you felt good about yourself as a result of grouping or backing up your support systems?

Finding a way to back up my child care coverage was a big relief for me. Establishing contact with alternate vendors let me stop worrying so much when the normal routines couldn't work—for whatever reason. And knowing that I had dependable people to turn to in a crisis gave me real peace of mind.

Potential Outcomes: What's the worst thing that could happen if you re-grouped your support system categories and improved your back-up plans now? What's the best thing that could happen?

The worst thing that could happen is that I could feel uncomfortable about admitting that I can't do it all on my own. But that's something I'm working on overcoming. And that's worth overcoming, since the best thing that could happen would be that I could end up with a much stronger support system and avert future problems.

Transformers

Talk-Over #1: How can you talk to yourself in a new way about what goes together that gives you a more flexible approach to getting the support you need?

I can say: "Regrouping my support system needs into basic categories will allow me to keep on top of the kinds of support I need and what I have to do to get it."

Talk-Over #2: How can you talk to yourself in a new way about your contingency plans that gives you a more flexible approach to getting the support you need?

I can say: "It's helpful to develop back-up systems whenever possible, especially for the systems that I rely on to deal with emergencies."

Conversation #74: Grouping And Backing Up Your Systems

Explorers

What Goes Together:

Contingency Plans:

Confidence-Builders

Life Lessons:

Potential Outcomes:

Transformers

Talk-Over #1:

Talk-Over #2:

Conversation #75: Surrounding Yourself With Positive People

Explorers

Assessing Attitudes: How would you characterize the dispositions of your professional and personal life allies?

My professional and personal life allies at the moment all are generally optimistic, upbeat, creative, and cooperative. Some of them tend also to be chronic worriers, however, and a couple are opinionated and domineering.

The Mirroring Effect: How do the dispositions of these people affect you?

Most of the time I feel energized by and relieved to have these people by my side. Occasionally, I feel agitated when dealing with their negative sides.

Confidence-Builders

Life Lessons: What three times have you felt good about yourself as a result of associating with positive people?

When I hosted a brunch for a few close friends who are really upbeat people; spent the day socializing with a working-mom mentor; and I devoted uninterrupted time to sharing tales of works-in-progress with my sister, I felt energized by associating with really upbeat people.

Potential Outcomes: What's the worst thing that could happen if you only included positive people in your inner circle now? What's the best thing that could happen?

The worst thing that could happen is that I'd feel the need to repress my honest feelings so I could always appear positive. The best thing would be that I would have an inner circle of visionary people who support the best in each other and encourage possibilities for personal and professional growth.

Transformers

Talk-Over #1: How can you talk to yourself in a new way about assessing attitudes that gives you a more flexible approach to getting the support you need?

I can say: "I can trust my impressions and instincts about people's attitudes, and it's important to be sure that I have truly positive people in my inner circle."

Talk-Over #2: How can you talk to yourself in a new way about the mirroring effect that gives you a more flexible approach to getting the support you need?

I can say: "When I closely associate with negative people, I feel turned off by the way they intensify already difficult situations. I need to remember that if these people are in my life, I'm exposing myself and my children to their negative attitudes and behavior."

Conversation #75: Surrounding Yourself With Positive People

Explorers

Assessing Attitudes:

The Mirroring Effect:

Confidence-Builders

Life Lessons:

Potential Outcomes:

Transformers

Talk-Over #1:

Talk-Over #2:

Conversation #76: Giving Up Martyrdom And Guessing Games

Explorers

The Martyr Complex: When do you generally ask for help: before you need it? On the spur of the moment? Never?

> I sometimes ask for help in advance, such as when I need child care coverage during a work or personal appointment in the future, or when I'm contemplating a career move and need advice. But more often I ask for help when I'm in a jam, because it's easier for me to give help than to ask for it.

Guessing Games: How do you usually ask for help? Do you ask directly? Wait patiently for somebody to offer? Drop hints?

> Nowadays I usually ask for help directly, though I usually soften my request by giving the other person the option of saying no if they find it too inconvenient to help out.

Confidence-Builders

Life Lessons: What three times have you felt good about yourself as a result of asking directly for help without feeling uncomfortable about it?

> Asking one of my mentors for career advice several months before my first child was born felt reassuring. And asking a busy colleague for feedback about a writing project at a critical stage was also rewarding. I'm also proud of the partnership I have with my husband, in which we regularly trade off home duties when the other's career requires more intense commitment for a time.

Potential Outcomes: What's the worst thing that could happen if you started asking for support as soon as you knew you needed it? What's the best thing that could happen?

> The worst thing that could happen is that I'd ask for help and then have to go back to somebody and say I really didn't need their help after all. The best thing would be that having contingency plans in place before a crisis struck would mean that I'd be less stressed and could avoid imposing on others at the last minute.

Transformers

Talk-Over #1: How can you talk to yourself in a new way about the martyr complex that gives you a more flexible approach to getting the support you need?

> I can say: "Asking for help doesn't mean I'm weak, and someone being unable to help is not a reflection on me, but on their own stressors."

Talk-Over #2: How can you talk to yourself in a new way about guessing games that gives you a more flexible approach to getting the support you need?

> I can say: "People appreciate a request for help that's made directly and respectfully. To hint at a need for help from someone generally leaves them feeling obligated, instead of willing."

Conversation #76: Giving Up Martyrdom And Guessing Games

Explorers

The Martyr Complex:

Guessing Games:

Confidence-Builders

Life Lessons:

Potential Outcomes:

Transformers

Talk-Over #1:

Talk-Over #2:

Conversation #77: Gathering Wisdom Hand-Me-Downs

Explorers

Eclectic Perspectives: Among the working moms you know that you can turn to for advice about support issues, how many different backgrounds and perspectives are available to you?

> In my family there are working moms in all the generations—their differences in age and experiences means that they each have something unique to offer me. The same is true about many of my friends, who have a wide range of different lifestyles and cultural backgrounds.

Storytelling 101: How many different ways can you learn about other working moms' support stories?

> I've found a lot of different ways to plug into the experiences of other working moms. For example, I've read about them and also talked to other working moms among my friends and acquaintances.

Confidence-Builders

Life Lessons: What three times have you felt good about yourself as a result of getting advice from other working moms with different backgrounds about support issues?

> When I was considering setting myself up with a home business, it was really helpful to ask for advice from another working mom who had made a similar choice. Listening to "what worked" and "what didn't" stories told by other working moms saved me a lot of time and trouble. And reading magazine articles about working moms inspired me to find creative solutions to my problems.

Potential Outcomes: What's the worst thing that could happen if you actively gathered advice about support issues from different types of working moms in various ways now? What's the best thing that could happen?

> The worst thing that could happen is that I might disagree with them or find the advice not applicable to my situation. The best thing would be that I'd have a wealth of support ideas to choose from and that I have the chance to connect with a lot of resourceful, intriguing working moms.

Transformers

Talk-Over #1: How can you talk to yourself in a new way about eclectic perspectives that gives you a more flexible approach to getting the support you need?

> I can say: "Seeking advice about support issues from other working moms with different backgrounds will expose me to a wide variety of innovative solutions that I can apply to my situation, and also allow me to form strong bonds with potential new allies."

Talk-Over #2: How can you talk to yourself in a new way about Storytelling 101 that gives you a more flexible approach to getting the support you need?

> I can say: "Learning about other working moms' support stories will not only expose me to new ideas, but will also give me inspiration and courage to create a lifestyle that works for me."

Conversation #77: Gathering Wisdom Hand-Me-Downs

Explorers

Eclectic Perspectives:

Storytelling 101:

Confidence-Builders

Life Lessons:

Potential Outcomes:

Transformers

Talk-Over #1:

Talk-Over #2:

Conversation #78: Using Your Life History As A Life Raft

Explorers

Inflating Your Raft: What ordinary or extraordinary challenges have you faced in your work or family lives at least in part by supporting yourself?

> When I decided to shed some excess weight and become stronger and more flexible, I enlisted the help of some experts in the field, but I mostly worked on my own. Dealing with my body image was a hard, scary challenge, and making it a priority was a turning point that has improved my life ever since.

Paddling Upstream: How can you apply the ways that you have faced challenges in the past to your current support needs as a working mom?

> I can take a disciplined approach to my support need priorities. I can research ways to meet my needs, and I can follow my instincts and let them lead me to a solution that feels right to me.

Confidence-Builders

Life Lessons: What three times have you felt good about yourself as a result of reviewing your personal heroine tales?

> Overcoming my struggle with my body image after my first child was born gave me a sense of empowerment. Looking back on how I handled redirecting my career and the financial implications gives me the strength to face my current challenges. I'm encouraged whenever I remember how I listened to my own intuitive signals about the direction of a writing project I was working on and ended up with a much stronger book.

Potential Outcomes: What's the worst thing that could happen if you regularly used your past success stories to become more self-reliant now? What's the best thing that could happen?

> The worst thing is that I relive old successes and never try something new. The best thing would be that my success stories remind me of strategies that worked for me in the past and give me the confidence to go after what I want.

Transformers

Talk-Over #1: How can you talk to yourself in a new way about inflating your raft that gives you a more flexible approach to getting the support you need?

> I can say: "Supporting myself is not an all-or-none proposition, and it's okay to get help from others when I need it—everybody needs a little help now and then."

Talk-Over #2: How can you talk to yourself in a new way about paddling upstream that gives you a more flexible approach to getting the support you need?

> I can say: "Important lessons in coping strategies can come from my personal heroine tales, but they are also precious sources of inspiration."

Conversation #78: Using Your Life History As A Life Raft

Explorers

Inflating Your Raft:

Paddling Upstream:

Confidence-Builders

Life Lessons:

Potential Outcomes:

Transformers

Talk-Over #1:

Talk-Over #2:

Conversation #79: Managing Your Assets

Explorers

A Balancing Act: Do your expenses typically exceed, equal, or fall short of your income? Why?

I usually manage to make ends meet, despite the high cost of living in the metropolitan New York area. That's mainly due to careful budgeting.

Showing Me the Money: How do you track your money? How do you handle your expenses? How about your taxes? And what about planning for the future?

I track my money using a software program, but I pay my bills by hand rather than electronically. I have an accountant to do my taxes. And, I have some savings and investments that I'm trying to build up for retirement, not to mention covering the cost of my kids' education when they reach college age.

Confidence-Builders

Life Lessons: What three times have you felt good about yourself as a result of living within your means, tracking and handling your income, or planning for the future?

I felt really good when I succeeded in launching my own business. Consulting with a professional to learn how to better plan for the future gave me confidence. Investing in good personal and business financial software has made it easier for me to develop and stick to a rational budget.

Potential Outcomes: What's the worst thing that could happen if you tried to manage your assets more effectively now? What's the best thing that could happen?

The worst thing that could happen is discovering that I can't justify some of my indulgences and that I'd have to cut back on spending that I really enjoy. On the other hand, the best thing that could happen is that I could find better ways to manage my assets and maximize my income.

Transformers

Talk-Over #1: How can you talk to yourself in a new way about balancing your income and expenses that gives you a more flexible approach to getting the support you need?

I can say: "I have options for maximizing my income to make my financial base even stronger by learning how to save more, invest more, earn more, or make the choice to move to a less expensive place. The choice is my own."

Talk-Over #2: How can you talk to yourself in a new way about "show me the money" that gives you a more flexible approach to getting the support you need?

I can say: "There's always room for improvement in how I handle my money and plan for the future. There is a wealth of advice out there from a variety of sources, including books, financial planners, accountants, and web sites."

Conversation #79: Managing Your Assets

Explorers

A Balancing Act:

Show Me the Money:

Confidence-Builders

Life Lessons:

Potential Outcomes:

Transformers

Talk-Over #1:

Talk-Over #2:

Conversation #80: Befriending Your Creative Muse

Explorers

Hosting a Playdate: What do you do to nurture your creativity?

> I find creative inspiration through reading, listening to music, dancing, communing with nature, meditating, and surfing the Internet.

Your Favorite Playgrounds: In what areas of your work and personal life do you feel most creative?

> I feel especially creative when I'm counseling others about choosing or managing their careers. Designing approaches for new books, making up silly songs for my children, matching movement to music, and visualizing ideas for decorating my house are also areas that give me a real creative boost.

Confidence-Builders

Life Lessons: What three times have you felt good about yourself as a result of exercising your creativity?

> I often work with clients who have complex, long-term career goals that have many paths to achieving them. Helping them figure out the best way to get there really makes me feel that I've done something worthwhile. When I created an interactive format for one of my book projects I got a powerful sense of accomplishment. And coming up with a series of personalized songs for my children to sing with me was very rewarding.

Potential Outcomes: What's the worst thing that could happen if you tried to be more creative in every aspect of your life? What's the best thing that could happen?

> The worst thing that could happen is that I'd feel performance pressure to be creatively "on" all the time, or that I can't follow the ideas through to completion. The best thing that could happen is that I'd learn to approach my life as whole in a fresher, more unusual way.

Transformers

Talk-Over #1: How can you talk to yourself in a new way about hosting a playdate that gives you a more flexible approach to getting the support you need?

> I can say: "By actively using the channels that connect me most directly to my muse, I can enter the creative zone faster and more frequently."

Talk-Over #2: How can you talk to yourself in a new way about your favorite playgrounds that gives you a more flexible approach to getting the support you need?

> I can say: "Creativity is not just about the fine arts, but also about everyday activities, and I may surprise myself by making wonderful new discoveries."

Conversation #80: Befriending Your Creative Muse

Explorers:

Hosting a Playdate:

Your Favorite Playgrounds:

Confidence-Builders

Life Lessons:

Potential Outcomes:

Transformers

Talk-Over #1:

Talk-Over #2:

Conversation #81: Approaching Your Challenges As Invitations

Explorers

Receiving the Invitation: What's your usual initial reaction to an overwhelming support challenge?

My usual initial reaction is to panic that I won't be able to handle it. At times like that I frequently feel all alone.

R.S.V.P.ing to Yourself: How do you recover from your initial negative reaction?

I try to talk myself through my concerns and options until I'm able to see the situation from a new perspective. Then I take a deep, cleansing breath and fully release the negativity.

Confidence-Builders

Life Lessons: What three times have you felt good about yourself as a result of coping emotionally with support challenges?

Once I had a tough time finding backup child care during a family crisis, but I handled it and felt very strong for having done so. Taking my daughter to pre-school the first time was hard on both of us, but I was proud of how I handled my emotions so her transition would be easier. I also feel good about the way I deal with the isolation, self-doubt, and rejection that are a part of the writing aspect of my career.

Potential Outcomes: What's the worst thing that could happen if you perceive support challenges as opportunities to become a stronger, more evolved person now? What's the best thing that could happen?

The worst thing that could happen is if I fail at finding opportunities in the challenges I face and just end up feeling as if I had failed. I could end up feeling weak and incompetent. But, by facing that fear, I could develop a more positive approach to life, and the problems that crop up would have less power to get me down or stress me out.

Transformers

Talk-Over #1: How can you talk to yourself in a new way about receiving the invitation that gives you a more flexible approach to getting the support you need?

I can say: "My support challenges are invitations to learn how I instinctively react to a stressful situation."

Talk-Over #2: How can you talk to yourself in a new way about R.S.V.P.ing to yourself that gives you a more flexible approach to getting the support you need?

I can say: "I acknowledge my initial negative reactions to some challenges, but I won't let those reactions stop me. After all, it's the process of bouncing back that ultimately determines what kind of working mom and person I'm becoming."

Conversation #81: Approaching Your Challenges As Invitations

Explorers

Receiving the Invitation:

R.S.V.P.ing to Yourself:

Confidence-Builders

Life Lessons:

Potential Outcomes:

Transformers

Talk-Over #1:

Talk-Over #2:

Conversation #82: Fostering Your Communities

Explorers

Work and Home Villages: What communities, or groups of people, are you a member of at work and in your personal life?

> The communities that I most closely identify with are my colleagues; my immediate family; my neighborhood; and my working-mom network of friends.

Role Playing: What support do you gain from your work and home communities? What support do you give to these communities?

> I gain support from and give support to my communities through the advice we give to one another, the active interest we take in each others' activities, the concern we show for each others' well-being, and the practical help we give each other in handling work and home issues.

Confidence-Builders

Life Lessons: What three times have you felt good about yourself as a result of gaining or giving support to your work and home communities?

> I've felt good about the support I've gotten from both my work and home communities since becoming a private practitioner. I also feel good about the support people have given me while I pursue my writing interests. And I feel good about the fact that my support community takes an active interest in my children's well-being.

Potential Outcomes: What's the worst thing that could happen if you fostered the development of your work and home communities? What's the best thing that could happen?

> The worst thing that could happen is that I'd have to sacrifice some privacy in order to give and get support. On the other hand, I could end up with mutually respectful, strong relationships with my work and home community members.

Transformers

Talk-Over #1: How can you talk to yourself about work and home villages that gives you a more flexible approach to getting the support you need?

> I can say: "I choose to help create a true sense of community—a sense of connection, mutual support, and responsibility, wherever I go and with any group that I find myself in."

Talk-Over #2: How can you talk to yourself about role playing that gives you a more flexible approach to getting the support you need?

> I can say: "My communities at work and home are great sources of support for me, when I actively work to strengthen them by giving freely in return."

Conversation #82: Fostering Your Communities

Explorers

Work and Home Villages:

Role Playing:

Confidence-Builders

Life Lessons:

Potential Outcomes:

Transformers

Talk-Over #1:

Talk-Over #2:

Conversation #83: Grounding Yourself In What's Meaningful

Explorers

The Heart of the Matter: What's meaningful to you in your work and family lives?

> What's meaningful to me is pursuing work that enables me to express my creative spirit and help others while sustaining loving, close relationships with my family that nurture our individual gifts, our feelings of security, our sense of belonging, and our self-esteem.

Making Memories: How do you remind yourself of what's meaningful when you're stressed out by support issues?

> I remind myself why I'm pursuing my work and what I love about being a mom. This lets me replace the feelings of anger, frustration, isolation, and sadness, with feelings of gratitude, love, and joy for the heart of my work and family lives.

Confidence-Builders

Life Lessons: What three times have you felt good about yourself as a result of focusing on what's meaningful to you in your work and family lives?

> I felt very good about redirecting my focus from the p's and q's of running my business to really look at why I was doing it. It was also good just to concentrate on writing the best books possible. It was truly liberating to stop second-guessing myself in all of the ambiguous situations related to my children—it freed me up to love and guide them to the best of my ability.

Potential Outcomes: What's the worst thing that could happen if you tried to reduce your stress by focusing on what's meaningful to you now? What's the best thing that could happen?

> The worst thing that could happen is that I could end up feeling more stressed out by how much is at stake if I don't work out my support issues. The best thing would be to find more patience and strength within myself to persevere in the search for resolutions to my support issues.

Transformers

Talk-Over #1: How can you talk to yourself about the heart of the matter that gives you a more flexible approach to getting the support you need?

> I can say: "I will seek support when I need it, even if I need help with mundane things, because support will help me grow, personally and professionally."

Talk-Over #2: How can you talk to yourself about making memories that gives you a more flexible approach to getting the support you need?

> I can say: "I will use tangible reminders of what's meaningful to me on all levels. I can reflect upon inspirational quotes; keep inspirational keepsakes nearby; and play music that inspires me."

Conversation #83: Grounding Yourself In What's Meaningful

Explorers

The Heart of the Matter:

Making Memories:

Confidence-Builders

Life Lessons:

Potential Outcomes:

Transformers

Talk-Over #1:

Talk-Over #2:

Conversation #84: Trusting The Process

Explorers

Changing Needs: How do you figure out what your support needs are and how they might evolve as a working mom?

I've used different methods to figure out my support needs and project how they might evolve. Some things I've tried are: keeping a log of support needs that come up over the course of a week; reading about other working moms' experiences; and talking with other working moms.

Invisible Guidance: How can you recognize untapped resources or hidden opportunities to meet your support needs?

I can continually ask myself whether something or someone might be a resource for my support needs, especially those things, people, or arrangements that I've never considered as resources before.

Confidence-Builders

Life Lessons: What three times have you felt good about yourself as a result of keeping up with your support needs or finding new resources to meet them?

I felt good about myself when I did a thorough job of researching how to run a home-based business as a working mom. I also felt good about finding other working moms who faced the same child-rearing issues I was coping with when my children were really little. Finally, I felt really good about being able to recognize that, as my family grew, so did my support needs.

Potential Outcomes: What's the worst thing that could happen if you trusted the process of recognizing and meeting your evolving needs now? What's the best thing that could happen?

The worst thing that could happen would be that I misjudge my needs or miss opportunities to meet them. The best thing would be that I become better and better at using an intuitive, low-stress approach to identifying my needs and finding ways to satisfy them.

Transformers

Talk-Over #1: How can you talk to yourself in a new way about changing needs that gives you a more flexible approach to getting the support you need?

I can say: "Since my support needs will continue to evolve, I need to stay flexible. I will trust the process of this evolution and embrace the changes as reflections of my own and others' growth."

Talk-Over #2: How can you talk to yourself in a new way about invisible guidance that gives you a more flexible approach to getting the support you need?

I can say: "As long as I stay optimistic and receptive, I'll attract people and possibilities to help me resolve them. I'll experience a deep sense of inner peace just by trusting the process."

Conversation #84: Trusting The Process

Explorers

Changing Needs:

Invisible Guidance:

Confidence-Builders

Life Lessons:

Potential Outcomes:

Transformers

Talk-Over #1:

Talk-Over #2:

ENERGY: Keeping On Going

9

The Conversations
  Living with double vision
  Listening to your whispers and screams
  Befriending your fears
  Forgiving yourself
  Respecting your natural cycles
  Shaking up your routine
  Plugging into stress outlets
  Harmonizing your relationships
  Hosting a comedy hour
  Transforming the usual into the unusual
  Rotating your activities
  Rewarding yourself for your achievements
  Remembering the basics
  Coming to all of your senses
  Minding your body and soul
  Becoming more self-ish

Working moms often have sapped our energy reserves by doing three things: by consistently prioritizing other people's needs ahead of their own; by ignoring their own natural tools and rhythms; and by holding onto negative emotions and experiences. The good news is that we can replace these draining practices with strategies that maximize our energy.

Putting Your Needs First

Working moms often put work and family tasks ahead of our personal needs. By doing so we receive payoffs like feeling needed by others and avoiding our own problems. But when you recognize that, as a working mom, you're already doing at least two jobs, you can clearly see that you deserve and need to rejuvenate yourself on a regular basis. Shaking up the parts of your routine that energize your mind, body, and spirit will prevent you from getting in a rut, or get you out of the one that you may already fallen into.

Similarly, using stress management techniques like visualization, affirmations, and massage may help you to maintain an even keel. Just focusing on the light side of life—and filling every day with hearty laughter—will make a difference. Perhaps most importantly, though, you can become more self-ish by shielding yourself from both external and internal energy drains, freeing up this energy to develop your natural gifts as fully as possible.

Through this process of developing your gifts, you'll gain energy. And by sharing these gifts with others, the energy you generate will come back to you in the forms of appreciation, enthusiasm, and inspiration for new directions for personal growth and community-building.

Tuning into Your Inner Wisdom

Working moms also frequently have ignored our instinctive needs and signals. With life moving at such a fast pace, it's easy to let the noise and demands of daily living drown out your own sense of what you need to do to accomplish your goals. And sometimes it seems that just about everybody has an opinion on how you should be handling your life—and that they're all too willing to "correct" your own choices for you.

Finding a lifestyle approach that is tailor-made for your own needs can be difficult. But you can learn to heed your intuition about potential problems—including energy meltdowns—and respect your natural energy cycles. When you tune in to what your own inner wisdom is telling you, you'll find it much easier to take advantage of your peak performance times as well as to meet your basic personal energy needs.

Sooner or Later You've Got to Let It Out!

As women, most of us have been culturally conditioned to deal with our negative emotions and experiences by holding them in, stuffing them away like an old pair of socks in the back of your dresser drawer to discard another time. But this approach clutters your psyche and depletes your energy reserves.

You can make room in your psyche's "drawer," by continually releasing your fears, forgiving yourself for your past mistakes, harmonizing your relationships, and finding creative ways to transform tedious tasks into bearable ones. And you can minimize the negative energy in your life by giving yourself meaningful rewards for your everyday as well as major achievements.

In the final chapter, you'll re-evaluate how you maintain and direct your energy. In each conversation you'll reconsider your current approach. In the process, you'll discover new ways to work and live with more vitality, maximizing your energy while fulfilling your responsibilities. And, as always, I'm still here talking with myself about these issues. So if you'd like some company during your conversations with yourself, pull up a chair and join me.

Conversation #85: Living With Double Vision

Explorers

Seeing Innies: When you review your daily "to do" list, how do you prioritize your personal needs among your work and family responsibilities?

> When I'm approaching my "to do" list with a balanced perspective, I put my most important personal needs above less important work and family tasks. But when I'm in "super working mom" mode, I find myself ranking all tasks as important, and when I'm tired, I find that I move my personal needs to the bottom of the list.

Watching Outies: What happens to your intellectual, emotional, and physical energy levels when you focus too much on others' needs at work and at home? What is the payoff when you over-focus on others?

> When I focus too much on others' needs, I begin to feel fuzzy brained, emotionally-drained, and physically tired. This leads to my playing the victim; avoiding my own problems and needs; claiming the self-sacrificing, martyr role; and feeling needed by others.

Confidence-Builders

Life Lessons: What three times have you felt good about yourself as a result of keeping your energy input and output balanced?

> When I downsized my private practice, took a writing sabbatical, and designated private time every day for rejuvenating myself I felt good about keeping my energy input and output balanced.

Potential Outcomes: What's the worst thing that could happen if you lived with double vision now? What's the best thing that could happen?

> The worst thing that could happen is that sometimes I might feel selfish for prioritizing my needs over others' needs. The best thing that could happen is that I maintain a more balanced flow of energy in and out of me.

Transformers

Talk-Over #1: How can you talk to yourself in a new way about seeing innies that gives you a more flexible approach to getting the energy you need?

> I can say: "As a working mom I'm already doing two jobs, so I deserve and need to rejuvenate myself."

Talk-Over #2: How can you talk to yourself in a new way about watching outies that gives you a more flexible approach to getting the energy you need?

> I can say: "I need to conserve energy by becoming aware of why I over-focus on others' needs and decide to nurture myself in positive ways."

Conversation #85: Living With Double Vision

Explorers

Seeing Innies:

Watching Outies:

Confidence-Builders

Life Lessons:

Potential Outcomes:

Transformers

Talk-Over #1:

Talk-Over #2:

Conversation #86: Listening To Your Whispers And Screams

Explorers

Basic Instincts: How do you first become aware of your intuition letting you know that something is wrong in your life? What do you do about it?

My intuition communicates with me first through a sensation somewhere in my body. I usually notice it and try to figure out what it means and, if I'm not sure, I ask myself what's up and wait for another signal.

Warning Signals: How do you become aware of your intuition letting you know something is really wrong? What do you do then?

When something is really wrong, I know because I get very strong physical sensations, and I usually hear my inner voice telling me to do something, like flee the scene or call someone. When this happens, I always heed my intuition.

Confidence-Builders

Life Lessons: What three times have you felt good about yourself as a result of listening to your intuition?

The first is the time that I decided not to pursue a potentially lucrative business venture with individuals whose ethics I questioned. The second is when I took a leap of faith to become an independent practitioner. The third is when I took my child to the doctor at my first inklings of an ear infection.

Potential Outcomes: What's the worst thing that could happen if you listened to your intuition more often and sooner now? What's the best thing that could happen?

The worst thing that could happen is that sometimes I might confuse my intuition with irrational concerns. The best thing that could happen is that I might begin to refine my ability to tune into my intuition which will help me enhance the quality of my life.

Transformers

Talk-Over #1: How can you talk to yourself in a new way about basic instincts that gives you a more flexible approach to getting the energy you need?

I can say: "When my instincts and intuition demand my attention, I will stop and listen to what they are trying to tell me."

Talk-Over #2: How can you talk to yourself in a new way about warning signals that gives you a more flexible approach to getting the energy you need?

I can say: "When I receive strong intuitive messages about negative scenarios, I can acknowledge that I might feel uneasy about these intuitions and still trust myself to respond to them even if I'm not exactly sure what may be a problem."

Conversation #86: Listening To Your Whispers And Screams

Explorers:

Basic Instincts:

Warning Signals:

Confidence-Builders

Life Lessons:

Potential Outcomes:

Transformers

Talk-Over #1:

Talk-Over #2:

Conversation #87: Befriending Your Fears

Explorers

Energy Sappers: What are some of your recurring fears as a working mom?

> I sometimes worry about failing as a worker or as a mom and about burning out at home or on the job.

Worry Charmers: How do you usually deal with your recurring fears?

> If I'm feeling brave, I'm likely to acknowledge my fears and let them go by addressing them. Other times, however, I'm liable to try to push them out of my mind. The first strategy seems to work the best, since once I give my fears a little attention, they seem to diminish. When I try to simply push them away, they keep coming back.

Confidence-Builders

Life Lessons: What three times have you felt good about yourself as a result of dealing with your recurring fears?

> I felt proud of myself when I faced my fear of failure and dared to start my own business. I felt empowered when I faced my fear of being abandoned when I became a home-based working mom. And when I overcame my fear of burning out by becoming the working mom of two children I felt relieved and energized.

Potential Outcomes: What's the worst thing that could happen if you befriended your old and new fears as soon as you met them now? What's the best thing that could happen?

> The worst thing that could happen is that I won't understand what they're trying to tell me about myself. The best thing that could happen is that I might finally break the habit of letting recurring fears consume my energy and direct my life.

Transformers

Talk-Over #1: How can you talk to yourself in a new way about energy sappers that gives you a more flexible approach to getting the energy you need?

> I can say: "My fears as a working mom are real, normal, and common among working moms."

Talk-Over #2: How can you talk to yourself in a new way about worry charmers that gives you a more flexible approach to getting the energy you need?

> I can say: "I have many options for minimizing my recurring fears. The key is to give myself the chance to meet and get to know my fears well enough to deal with them."

Conversation #87: Befriending Your Fears

Explorers

Energy Sappers:

Worry Charmers:

Confidence-Builders

Life Lessons:

Potential Outcomes:

Transformers

Talk-Over #1:

Talk-Over #2:

Conversation #88: Forgiving Yourself

Explorers

Holding On: How do you hold onto past mistakes you've made at work and at home? How does holding onto past mistakes affect your energy level?

> Sometimes I watch reruns in my mind's eye, or re-experience conversations about them, but usually I replay and analyze conversations. Each time I replay and analyze a conversation, I drain my energy level a little more.

Letting Go: How do you handle the possibility of similar mistakes in the future?

> Sometimes I try to avoid situations where similar mistakes could occur. As I continue to mature, I find myself most often just trying again, expecting the best—and it often turns out okay because of my positive attitude.

Confidence-Builders

Life Lessons: What three times have you felt good about yourself as a result of forgiving yourself for your mistakes at work and at home?

> When I forgave myself for double-booking work appointments one day; forgetting to pick up the dry cleaning when it was my turn; and deleting a set of e-mails before I read them, I felt good about not berating myself or holding onto these mistakes.

Potential Outcomes: What's the worst thing that could happen if you made it a priority to release yourself from the bondage of past mistakes now? What's the best thing that could happen?

> The worst thing that could happen is that I might repeat my mistakes because I haven't taken the time to figure out why I made them. The best thing that could happen is that I live most often in the present, rather than the past.

Transformers

Talk-Over #1: How can you talk to yourself in a new way about holding on that gives you a more flexible approach to getting the energy you need?

> I can say: "Living in the past won't undo my mistakes—it just weighs me down and drains me of the energy I need for living in the present."

Talk-Over #2: How can you talk to yourself in a new way about letting go that gives you a more flexible approach to getting the energy you need?

> I can say: "To prepare for facing situations like the ones I've made mistakes in before, I can make sure I've made amends for the previous situations by apologizing to anyone affected by my mistake and fixing the problem as much as possible."

Conversation #88: Forgiving Yourself

Explorers:

Holding On:

Letting Go:

Confidence-Builders

Life Lessons:

Potential Outcomes:

Transformers

Talk-Over #1:

Talk-Over #2:

Conversation #89: Respecting Your Natural Cycles

Explorers

Riding the Highs: When during the day do you typically have high energy? How do you take advantage of these peak performance times in your work and personal life?

I normally have high energy first thing in the morning and late at night, when I get a second wind. I take advantage of these times by saving my most intellectually and physically challenging tasks to do when I'm at my peak.

Waiting Out the Lows: When typically do you have low energy during the day? How do you get through these low energy periods in your work and personal lives?

My low energy periods are usually in the mid-afternoon and early evening. I can deal with them most effectively by taking a brisk walk, eating a healthy snack, or taking a brief nap. Sometimes, though, I resort to eating junk food and plowing through whatever tasks are at hand. The problem is that I'm usually unproductive when I try to do this.

Confidence-Builders

Life Lessons: What three times have you felt good about yourself as a result of respecting your natural energy cycles?

When I worked on challenging sections of my last book first thing in the morning or late at night I was always very pleased with how those sections turned out. I also felt good after I started planning a healthy snack and water break with my kids during my mid-afternoon slump time and when I started keeping a regular wind-down time in the early evening during the dinner-bath-bedtime blitz.

Potential Outcomes: What's the worst thing that could happen if you maximized your low as well as high energy cycles now? What's the best thing that could happen?

The worst thing that could happen is that I might get less work and housework done each day. The best thing that could happen is that I could feel more balanced overall, and less cranky during my low times.

Transformers

Talk-Over #1: How can you talk to yourself in a new way about riding the highs that gives you a more flexible approach to getting the energy you need?

I can say: "There are numerous benefits to saving my most difficult tasks for my high-energy cycles. Also, I can make sure that I don't overdo it during these peak-performance times so that I don't feel especially exhausted during my low cycles."

Talk-Over #2: How can you talk to yourself in a new way about waiting out the lows that gives you a more flexible approach to getting the energy you need?

I can say: "I will make a list of the things I can do to fortify myself during my low energy cycles, so that I can remind myself what to do when my energy levels get low."

Conversation #89: Respecting Your Natural Cycles

Explorers

Riding the Highs:

Waiting Out the Lows:

Confidence-Builders

Life Lessons:

Potential Outcomes:

Transformers

Talk-Over #1:

Talk-Over #2:

Conversation #90: Shaking Up Your Routine

Explorers

Varying Your Habits: What daily patterns can you alter to give yourself a different experience—just for the fun of it?

I can alter the route I take to and from work. I can change the way I schedule my usual workday tasks. And I can add a little variety to what I eat. I can also alter how I spend my free time with my family.

Spin-Off Energizers: In addition to giving you energy directly, what are some indirect benefits of varying your routine?

Varying my routine can indirectly increase my energy by helping me become more aware of my transitions in and out of work mode. It can also help me discover ways to manage my time more efficiently.

Confidence-Builders

Life Lessons: What three times have you felt good about yourself as a result of shaking up your routine?

When I varied my exercise routine; experimented with a new haircut and clothing style; and changed the order in which I did my work for the day, shaking up my routine made me feel invigorated.

Potential Outcomes: What's the worst thing that could happen if you experimented with shaking up new parts of your routine now? What's the best thing that could happen?

The worst thing that could happen is that I might shake up too many things at once and feel disoriented. The best thing that could happen is that I could feel a renewed interest in my life and that I could become more interesting to others.

Transformers

Talk-Over #1: How can you talk to yourself in a new way about varying your habits that gives you a more flexible approach to getting the energy you need?

I can say: "It's possible to change parts of my daily routine to boost my energy, while still maintaining enough structure and consistency overall that I know what to expect and can still enjoy important rituals."

Talk-Over #2: How can you talk to yourself in a new way about spin-off energizers that gives you a more flexible approach to getting the energy you need?

I can say: "It's important to shake up the parts of my routine that energize my mind, body, and spirit regularly, both to prevent getting in a rut and to get out of one."

Conversation #90: Shaking Up Your Routine

Explorers

Varying Your Habits:

Spin-Off Energizers:

Confidence-Builders

Life Lessons:

Potential Outcomes:

Transformers

Talk-Over #1:

Talk-Over #2:

Conversation #91: Plugging Into Stress Outlets

Explorers

Recharging Your Battery: What stress management techniques do you currently use? How often do you use each of them?

> At least twice a day I use visualization, progressive muscle relaxation, massage, music, or affirmations.

Adding Extension Cords: What other techniques appeal to you? How could you explore these options?

> Techniques like biofeedback and meditation appeal to me. I could head down to the local bookstore to find a manual, audio-casette, or videotape to try to learn more about them. I could also sign up for a class or workshop or look for information on the Internet.

Confidence-Builders

Life Lessons: What three times have you felt good about yourself as a result of using stress management techniques?

> Using deep breathing to relax before teaching a workshop; progressive muscle relaxation as a pre-bedtime ritual; and affirmations in the morning to start my day have all made me feel more relaxed and centered.

Potential Outcomes: What's the worst thing that could happen if you plugged into stress outlets more regularly and explored new ones now? What's the best thing that could happen?

> The worst thing that could happen is that I could find out that I'm not very good at some new technique I try to learn. The best thing would be that de-stressing becomes such an integral part of my daily routine that I raise my stress threshold and become a more relaxed, easygoing person most of the time.

Transformers

Talk-Over #1: How can you talk to yourself in a new way about recharging your battery that gives you a more flexible approach to getting the energy you need?

> I can say: "Using stress management techniques consistently is the key to keeping my energy level high. When I'm tempted to slack off using them because I'm busy or feeling lazy, I can remind myself that this is when I need them the most."

Talk-Over #2: How can you talk to yourself in a new way about adding extension cords that gives you a more flexible approach to getting the energy you need?

> I can say: "Learning new stress management techniques can be fun and rewarding. By exploring new techniques, I add variety to my life at the same time that I'm making myself a stronger, more resilient person."

Conversation #91: Plugging Into Stress Outlets

Explorers

Recharging Your Battery:

Adding Extension Cords:

Confidence-Builders

Life Lessons:

Potential Outcomes:

Transformers

Talk-Over #1:

Talk-Over #2:

Conversation #92: Harmonizing Your Relationships

Explorers

Keeping the Peace: What steps do you currently take to promote peaceful relationships at work and at home?

> I try to think before I speak; offer others my support; and respect others' opinions even when they differ from my own.

Reacting to Conflicts: How do you currently deal with tension and conflict in your relationships at work and at home?

> Sometimes I confront others; other times I bend and compromise; or I'll pull back from the relationship until I can set different relationship boundaries.

Confidence-Builders

Life Lessons: What three times have you felt good about yourself as a result of harmonizing your relationships?

> It felt good to pull back when work on my book was going a little slowly. By letting myself cool down, I had a chance to really work out what I wanted my editor to do. Taking a break from socializing with a domineering friend for a while gave me a chance to set new boundaries on our relationship so that I felt less pressure from her. And, when I finally confronted my husband about a problem that had been causing tension between us, our relationship was greatly improved.

Potential Outcomes: What's the worst thing that could happen if you pro-actively as well as reactively managed your relationships better now? What's the best thing that could happen?

> The worst thing that could happen is that, instead of improving harmony, I could inadvertently create more tension in my relationships. The best thing would be that, by reducing the conflict in my life, I could end up feeling more peaceful, and my relationships could give me more energy for my day-to-day living.

Transformers

Talk-Over #1: How can you talk to yourself in a new way about keeping the peace that gives you a more flexible approach to getting the energy you need?

> I can say: "Most of the time, the people in my life are doing the best they can, and I shouldn't be judgmental when people do things differently than I would."

Talk-Over #2: How can you talk to yourself in a new way about reacting to conflicts that gives you a more flexible approach to getting the energy you need?

> I can say: "My reaction to conflict will be different in each situation, depending on the strength of my feelings about the situation, my history with the person that I'm in conflict with, and even my stress level at the time."

Conversation #92: Harmonizing Your Relationships

Explorers

Keeping the Peace:

Reacting to Conflicts:

Confidence-Builders

Life Lessons:

Potential Outcomes:

Transformers

Talk-Over #1:

Talk-Over #2:

Conversation #93: Hosting A Comedy Hour

Explorers

The Lighter Sides: What makes you laugh at work and at home?

> Listening to friends tell jokes; watching funny television shows and movies; reading funny books; and playing self-trivia games.

Partners in Comedy: To whom do you turn when you get too intense about your life at work and at home?

> I turn to my husband and a couple of my close friends to share a laugh.

Confidence-Builders

Life Lessons: What three times have you felt good about yourself as a result of exercising your sense of humor to maintain perspective?

> When I spent an hour with a colleague brainstorming the most outrageously funny, worst-case scenarios for carrying out a business idea; when I took a comedy break after a tough day on the home front by watching an old, funny movie with my husband; and when I swapped sitcom-worthy work and family life stories with a close friend, I felt rejuvenated.

Potential Outcomes: What's the worst thing that could happen if you lightened up regularly and found partners in comedy now? What's the best thing that could happen?

> The worst thing that could happen is that I could have trouble shaking myself out of a funk. The best thing that could happen is that I could grow my sense of humor and that it makes not only my life, but the lives of those around me more fun and energized.

Transformers

Talk-Over #1: How can you talk to yourself in a new way about the lighter sides that gives you a more flexible approach to getting the energy you need?

> I can say: "It's good for me to laugh as much as possible with others, at my own quirks, and the everyday oddities that we all encounter in life, because laughter releases my tension and gives me more energy."

Talk-Over #2: How can you talk to yourself in a new way about partners in comedy that gives you a more flexible approach to getting the energy you need?

> I can say: "I will make 'laughter dates' with my family and friends to make sure I have enough fun in my life."

Conversation #93: Hosting A Comedy Hour

Explorers

The Lighter Sides:

Partners in Comedy:

Confidence-Builders

Life Lessons:

Potential Outcomes:

Transformers

Talk-Over #1:

Talk-Over #2:

Conversation #94: Transforming The Usual Into The Unusual

Explorers

Ordinary Stuff: What tasks at work and home are especially tedious, yet necessary parts of your daily routine?

Some especially tedious, yet necessary, tasks are filing, paying bills, doing laundry, washing dishes, and taking out the garbage.

Energy Reserves: How do you make these tasks bearable?

Sometimes I'll do the most tedious chores first thing in the morning. Sometimes I'll just make a list of all the dull tasks I've got to do and tackle them all at once so they're out of the way. Sometimes I'll just rush through them. And sometimes I give myself some kind of reward.

Confidence-Builders

Life Lessons: What three times have you felt good about yourself as a result of making energy downer tasks into energy upper experiences?

I felt good about myself when I grouped together my necessary housework and errands and took care of them all before 10:00 a.m. When I simplified my financial record-keeping system both for my business and my personal life it really boosted my sense of efficiency. And I really enjoyed it when I rewarded myself for catching up on my business and personal filing by taking a break to read a novel.

Potential Outcomes: What's the worst thing that could happen if you approached your mundane tasks from a new perspective now? What's the best thing that could happen?

The worst thing that could happen is that I'd discover that these tasks still were pretty tedious. The best thing that could happen is that the time I spend doing these tasks becomes a more meaningful experience.

Transformers

Talk-Over #1: How can you talk to yourself in a new way about ordinary stuff that gives you a more flexible approach to getting the energy you need?

I can say: "By zeroing in first on my most annoying tasks at work and home I can find creative ways to do them that will make them less tedious."

Talk-Over #2: How can you talk to yourself in a new way about energy reserves that gives you a more flexible approach to getting the energy you need?

I can say: "I'll transform my routine tasks into not just tolerable, but worthwhile, activities by kidding around, talking with a friend, and reflecting on my life while I'm doing them."

Conversation #94: Transforming The Usual Into The Unusual

Explorers

Ordinary Stuff:

Energy Reserves:

Confidence-Builders

Life Lessons:

Potential Outcomes:

Transformers

Talk-Over #1:

Talk-Over #2:

Conversation #95: Rotating Your Activities

Explorers

Move It or Lose It: What activities in your work and personal life do you rotate from time to time to keep your interest and energy levels up?

> I rotate my work projects, leisure time activities, and family rituals to keep my interest and energy levels up.

Choice Versus Chance: Which activities do you rotate by choice and which activities do you rotate by chance or circumstance?

> I rotate hosting dinners for friends, work projects, and family rituals by choice, and rotate seasonal outdoor activities and preparing family dinners with my husband by chance or circumstance.

Confidence-Builders

Life Lessons: What three times have you felt good about yourself as a result of rotating your activities?

> It felt good to take a writing sabbatical in order to concentrate on new book projects. When our schedules made it difficult to keep old family rituals, it was fun to get together with my family to create new ones. And when I felt I was getting into a rut, I tried getting into new seasonal sports and really enjoyed myself.

Potential Outcomes: What's the worst thing that could happen if you chose to rotate selected work and personal activities more frequently now? What's the best thing that could happen?

> The worst thing that could happen is that I shift gears too much and too fast. The best thing that could happen is that I rotate my activities just enough to keep me feeling simulated and energized.

Transformers

Talk-Over #1: How can you talk to yourself in a new way about move it or lose it that gives you a more flexible approach to getting the energy you need?

> I can say: "It's o.k. to select activities from all areas of my work and personal lives to rotate, as long as I remember to respect the fact that certain activities are important to keep me grounded."

Talk-Over #2: How can you talk to yourself in a new way about choice versus chance that gives you a more flexible approach to getting the energy you need?

> I can say: "Timing is important when I'm choosing to rotate my activities: Too much change too often can deplete, rather than replenish my energy, and too little change too infrequently can have the same effect."

Conversation #95: Rotating Your Activities

Explorers

Move It or Lose It:

Choice Versus Chance:

Confidence-Builders

Life Lessons:

Potential Outcomes:

Transformers

Talk-Over #1:

Talk-Over #2:

Conversation #96: Rewarding Yourself For Your Achievements

Explorers

Good Doings: What do you consider to be achievements in your work and family life?

In my work life I usually think of achievements as completing major projects, and in my family life I usually think of achievements as helping my children to feel good about themselves and learn new life skills.

Honoring Yourself: How do you reward yourself for your accomplishments?

I do things like praising myself; going out for a special meal; taking some time off; taking a trip; and buying myself something special, like a pen or new outfit.

Confidence-Builders

Life Lessons: What three times have you felt good about yourself as a result of giving yourself something for your triumphs?

When I successfully taught a new workshop I bought myself a new work outfit as a reward for my success. After completing my last book project I took time out to celebrate a job well done. When I helped my children to feel good about themselves, I shared my happiness with my husband and other family members over a special meal.

Potential Outcomes: What's the worst thing that could happen if you expanded your definition of "achievement" and improved your reward system now? What's the best thing that could happen?

The worst thing that could happen is that I get more caught up in the reward than in the value of the achievement itself. The best thing that could happen is that I recognize the range of my achievements and nurture myself as a capable working mom.

Transformers

Talk-Over #1: How can you talk to yourself in a new way about good doings that gives you a more flexible approach to getting the energy you need?

I can say: "I achieve many things every day that I may take for granted as ordinary, but that are actually significant."

Talk-Over #2: How can you talk to yourself in a new way about honoring yourself that gives you a more flexible approach to getting the energy you need?

I can say: "Before beginning a new task, I can talk to myself about the reward I will deserve upon its completion."

Conversation #96: Rewarding Yourself For Your Achievements

Explorers

Good Doings:

Honoring Yourself:

Confidence-Builders

Life Lessons:

Potential Outcomes:

Transformers

Talk-Over #1:

Talk-Over #2:

Conversation #97: Remembering The Basics

Explorers

Caretaking Do's and Don'ts: What personal, basic energy needs do you consistently take care of at work and at home? What needs do you consistently neglect?

> I consistently eat well, challenge my intellect, find beauty and meaning in the world, feel connected to others and nature, and nurture hope. Instead of formal exercise, I get my work-out while playing with my children, taking walks with them, and doing housework. I'm not very consistent about how much sleep I get and when I get it.

Prioritizing Holistic Living: How do you or could you prioritize meeting your basic energy needs?

> I could get my children involved in my regular exercise sessions. I could get into the habit of carrying a water bottle with me wherever I go and keeping healthy snacks readily available in the refrigerator. I could read a chapter of a book before bed; take a nature walk every weekend; and take cat naps or at least really relax whenever I get the chance.

Confidence-Builders

Life Lessons: What three times have you felt good about yourself as a result of meeting your basic energy needs?

> There was a stretch there when I got up early several days in a week to exercise before my children woke up and before I started to work and I was energized to face the day. It felt good when I managed to plan and prepare a week of healthy dinners ahead of time. And I was proud of myself for taking naps while my children did when I needed them.

Potential Outcomes: What's the worst thing that could happen if you committed yourself to living more holistically now? What's the best thing that could happen?

> The worst thing that could happen is that I have trouble finding ways to meet all of my basic needs all of the time. The best thing that could happen is that I meet more of my basic needs more of the time than before and am a healthier, more energized person.

Transformers

Talk-Over #1: How can you talk to yourself in a new way about caretaking do's and don'ts that gives you a more flexible approach to getting the energy you need?

> I can say: "It always feels good when I've made the effort to take care of myself."

Talk-Over #2: How can you talk to yourself in a new way about prioritizing holistic living that gives you a more flexible approach to getting the energy you need?

> I can say: "My needs are not just physical—I need to pay attention to my intellectual, emotional, and spiritual selves as well."

Conversation #97: Remembering The Basics

Explorers

Caretaking Do's and Don'ts:

Prioritizing Holistic Living:

Confidence-Builders

Life Lessons:

Potential Outcomes:

Transformers

Talk-Over #1:

Talk-Over #2:

Conversation #98: Coming To All Of Your Senses

Explorers

Common Senses: Which of your senses (including your sense of intuition) do you enjoy stimulating regularly? What senses do you tend to ignore, either intentionally or unintentionally?

> I gravitate toward stimulating my senses of sight, hearing, touch, and intuition regularly. I sometimes unintentionally forget to nurture my senses of smell and taste.

Sensory Wake-Ups: How can you awaken each of your senses to boost your energy level?

> I can awaken my sense of sight by viewing an art exhibit; my sense of hearing by attending a concert; my sense of smell by practicing aromatherapy; my sense of taste by indulging in a favorite meal; my sense of touch by getting a massage; and my sense of intuition by following my instincts.

Confidence-Builders

Life Lessons: What three times have you felt good about yourself as a result of fully engaging one of your senses?

> I really enjoy it whenever I let my intuition guide me throughout the day on an adventure of exploring new places, people, and things.

Potential Outcomes: What's the worst thing that could happen if you came to all of your senses now? What's the best thing that could happen?

> The worst thing that could happen is that I could experience sensory overload. The best thing is that I could feel more alive and appreciate new dimensions of my work and family lives.

Transformers

Talk-Over #1: How can you talk to yourself in a new way about common senses that gives you a more flexible approach to getting the energy you need?

> I can say: "I need to remind myself of specific things that satisfy my senses."

Talk-Over #2: How can you talk to yourself in a new way about sensory wake-ups that gives you a more flexible approach to getting the energy you need?

> I can say: "I need to remind myself of the small pleasures that are around me every day."

Conversation #98: Coming To All Of Your Senses

Explorers

Common Senses:

Sensory Wake-Ups:

Confidence-Builders

Life Lessons:

Potential Outcomes:

Transformers

Talk-Over #1:

Talk-Over #2:

Conversation #99: Minding Your Body And Soul

Explorers

Soul Searching: How does your soul communicate with you when your energy is out of balance or depleted?

> When my energy is out of balance or in short supply I tend to focus more on the negative than the positive side of people and situations.

Desperately Seeking Energy: What happens to you when you disregard your soul's early warnings about an impending energy meltdown?

> I have a pessimistic viewpoint most of the time; I argue more with others; I tend to catch colds; and I isolate myself more often.

Confidence-Builders

Life Lessons: What three times have you felt good about yourself as a result of paying attention to your soul's warnings about your decreasing energy?

> When I was exhausted by a draining work environment, I felt good about being able to recognize what was happening and taking steps to get over it. After I my first child was born I tended to overwork myself, but it felt good when I recognized the warning signs and got some help. And recently I realized I needed more chunks of time to express myself creatively through my work, letting me pay attention to my soul's warnings about my decreasing energy.

Potential Outcomes: What's the worst thing that could happen if you minded your body and soul now? What's the best thing that could happen?

> The worst thing that could happen is that I'll need to slow down or otherwise change my lifestyle to restore my energy. The best thing that could happen is that I avert energy meltdowns and learn to balance my energy on a regular basis.

Transformers

Talk-Over #1: How can you talk to yourself in a new way about soul searching that gives you a more flexible approach to getting the energy you need?

> I can say: "It's in my best interests for me to notice the signals, listen to the messages, and fully experience the feelings and sensations that occur when my soul is communicating with me about problems with my energy flow."

Talk-Over #2: How can you talk to yourself in a new way about desperately seeking energy that gives you a more flexible approach to getting the energy you need?

> I can say: "I'll reinterpret the unpleasant experiences I have when I ignore my soul's early warnings about an energy meltdown as my way of sabotaging myself, forcing myself to restore my energy."

Conversation #99: Minding Your Body And Soul

Explorers

Soul Searching:

Desperately Seeking Energy:

Confidence-Builders

Life Lessons:

Potential Outcomes:

Transformers

Talk-Over #1:

Talk-Over #2:

Conversation #100: Becoming More Self-ish

Explorers

The Energy Shield: How do you protect yourself from energy drains at work and at home?

> I devote time every day to nurturing myself and try to set clear boundaries and limits to prevent overextending myself.

Expressing Yourself: How do you develop your natural gifts as fully as possible?

> I explore different interests; read books about them; befriend others with similar interests; and devote regular time to enjoying them.

Confidence-Builders

Life Lessons: What three times have you felt good about yourself as a result of becoming more self-ish?

> When I pared down the number of commitments in my life as a whole to focus on the most important ones I felt empowered and energized. When I began making it a must to set aside time every day to nurture myself, I discovered that I was less likely to feel stressed out even after a hard day's work. And when I devoted regular time to developing my natural gifts, I felt good about becoming more self-ish.

Potential Outcomes: What's the worst thing that could happen if you became even more self-ish now? What's the best thing that could happen?

> The worst thing that could happen is that people might think I'm selfishly ignoring their needs because they're used to being the center of my attention. The best thing would be for my family and friends to discover how much everybody benefits from the increased energy and growth I'll gain by becoming more self-ish.

Transformers

Talk-Over #1: How can you talk to yourself in a new way about the energy shield gives you a more flexible approach to getting the energy you need?

> I can say: "I'll take responsibility for what drains my energy both at work and at home by establishing clearer boundaries with others, and by taking better care of myself by nurturing my mind, body, and spirit every day."

Talk-Over #2: How can you talk to yourself in a new way about expressing yourself that gives you a more flexible approach to getting the energy you need?

> I can say: "Through the process of developing my gifts, I gain energy. And by sharing these gifts with others, the energy I generate comes back to me as well as to still others in the forms of appreciation, enthusiasm, and inspiration for new directions for personal growth and community-building."

Conversation #100: Becoming More Self-ish

Explorers

The Energy Shield:

Expressing Yourself:

Confidence-Builders

Life Lessons:

Potential Outcomes:

Transformers

Talk-Over #1:

Talk-Over #2:

APPENDIX: THE CONVERSATIONS

Identity: Integrating Your Selves

Support: Making It After All

Energy: Keeping On Going

ABOUT THE AUTHOR

Marci Taub, M.A., a career counselor specializing in work-life balance issues, is president of Careerstyling®, L.L.C., a seminar and consulting company (www.careerstyling.com). She is the author of *Job Notes: Interviews* (1997), and the co-author of *Job Smart: What You Need to Know to Get the Job You Want* (1997) and *Work Smart: 250 Smart Moves Your Boss Already Knows* (1998), all published by Random House/Princeton Review Books. Marci has been sourced on career issues in several major media, including *The Los Angeles Times, The Washington Post, Redbook, Shape, Cosmopolitan, Mademoiselle, Glamour,* and *Teen People*. Her background includes career development services in private practice, higher education, and corporate human resources. Marci holds a B.A. from Oberlin College, an M.A. in Counseling from Montclair State University, and a Certificate in Adult Career Planning and Development from New York University. She is a member of the American Counseling Association, the National Career Development Association, and the Career Masters Institute.

Marci is also a working mom. She resides in New Jersey with her husband and their two children.

Careerstyling® and Interview Yourself™ are trademarks of Careerstyling®, L.L.C.

IT'S YOUR

LIFE SO

LIVE IT

YOUR WAY